STAR WARS

THE PADAWAN COOKBOOK

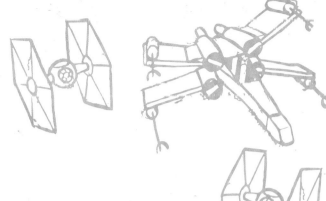

STAR WARS

THE PADAWAN COOKBOOK

KID-FRIENDLY RECIPES FROM A GALAXY FAR, FAR AWAY

By Jenn Fujikawa and Liz Lee Heinecke

INSIGHT
EDITIONS

SAN RAFAEL · LOS ANGELES · LONDON

CONTENTS

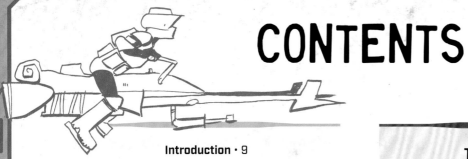

INTRODUCTION

> *" Pass on what you have learned. "*
>
> — Yoda

I started creating *Star Wars* recipes because I wanted my kids to see how much fun food can be. By making meals from scratch as themed food with characters that they know and love, I hoped that they'd be more willing to be adventurous and try new things.

The *Star Wars* universe is a vast, creative place, full of inspiration. Whether a favorite droid, planet, or creature, seeing something familiar on a plate will always bring a smile. All generations can connect to *Star Wars* adventures, which makes sharing the experience of making food exciting for all ages.

Every Padawan learner must complete the Jedi Trials to become a Jedi Knight. As a nod to that Jedi tradition, this book offers a journey for culinary Padawans who want to learn more about the kitchen. Each trial features a full meal, so that each section is its own complete story. Starting out with the simplest no-cook recipes in the first trial, each section escalates in difficulty, so that Padawans can level up to using the oven and stove, and eventually feel confident in making a whole meal.

There's no harm in staying in the lower levels of the trials. Taking time to hone skills is the best way to become a Jedi master in the kitchen. If you make a mistake, don't worry. Understanding that these stumbles sometimes happen is all a part of the cooking experience.

Most of all, these recipes are for families to learn together. Parents should supervise the use of knives and heat for safety purposes and act as guides at all times to help along the way. It's all a part of the process of learning and feeling comfortable in the kitchen.

Let the *Star Wars* universe guide you and take you on a cooking adventure. Have fun, be creative, make mistakes, and most importantly, be proud of creating something you can share with family and friends. Enjoy your time in the kitchen, and may the Force be with you.

Jenn Fujikawa

KITCHEN TOOLS

BOX GRATER	**COLANDER**	**DRY MEASURING CUPS**
Shreds foods such as cheese or grates the skin off citrus fruits (aka, zest)	Drains liquids through the small holes that cover the bowl	Helps you determine larger amounts of ingredients
FRYING PAN	**IMMERSION BLENDER**	**LADLE**
Useful for frying foods or for general cooking use	A handheld machine that can turn foods into a puree	Great for serving soups or stews
LIQUID MEASURING CUP	**MEASURING SPOONS**	**MINI CHOPPER**
Useful for determining exact amounts of liquids, by lining up the top of a liquid to the marks on the glass	Helps you determine smaller amounts of ingredients	A machine that chops small foods and ingredients like herbs. Not to be confused with a smaller version of the droid also known as C1-10P.
ROLLING PIN	**RUBBER SPATULA**	**SAUCEPAN WITH LID**
Flattens or rolls out dough	Used to fold ingredients into each other, or scrape the sides of bowls	Useful for boiling or simmering foods
SPATULA	**STAND MIXER**	**WHISK**
Helpful for flipping or turning foods during the cooking process	A machine that mixes, beats, or whips foods at varying speeds	Smoothly mixes or whips liquids and batters

DIETARY CONSIDERATIONS

GF = Gluten Free | V = Vegetarian | V+ = Vegan

Item	GF	V	V+
BANTHA MILK SLUSHIE	GF	V	V+
PADAWAN TRAINER SPIRALS		V	
SNOWDRIFT SAUCE	GF	V	
FRUIT AND CHEESE LIGHTSABER SKEWERS	GF	V	
OMEGA'S POPCORN MIX	GF	V	
PASAANA POPS	GF	V	
TWIN SUNS TOAST		V	
GROGU'S AVOCADO DIP		V	
CRIMSON DAWN COOLER	GF	V	V+
YODA'S ILUM SNOW CHURN	GF	V	V+
HERA'S MEILOORUN SMOOTHIE	GF	V	V+
MUDHORN EGG NOODLES			
JAWA SUSHI		V	
ANAKIN'S BOONTA EVE COB	GF	V	
DARTH VADER'S MUSTAFAR FRUIT CUPS	GF	V	
CHOPPER CHEESE TOAST			
SITH SOUPERS	GF	V	V+
MOOF MILK PARFAIT	GF	V	
GINGER "SNAP" WEXLEYS		V	
RED FIVE'S REFRESHMENT	GF	V	V+
R2-KT RICE BALLS	GF		
BLURRG FEED		V	
ENDOR ROLLS	GF		
TAKODANA SALAD	GF	V	V+
BUTTER CHEWIES	GF	V	
MAUL CAKES		V	V+
MON CALA PARCELS	GF		

Item	GF	V	V+
BATUUAN GARLIC GRAINS	GF	V	V+
AHSOKA'S JELLY CUBES	GF		
BESPIN BREW	GF	V	
LUKE SKYWALKER'S AHCH-TO SMOOTHIE	GF	V	V+
PASTRY PUFFER PIGS			
NERF NUGGETS			
JOGAN FRUIT PUFFS		V	
STORMTROOPER DONUTS		V	
STARKILLER ICE TWIST	GF	V	
MYNOCK WINGS	GF		
JEDI OUTPOST TUBERS	GF	V	V+
FRUIT TIE FIGHTERS	GF	V	V+
LOTH-CAT COOKIES	GF	V	
BOBA'S BOBA	GF	V	V+
BB-8 SLURRY	GF	V	
JAR JAR'S JACKFRUIT STEW	GF	V	V+
PADAWAN BRAIDED BREAD		V	
"MAY THE FILLING BE WITH YOU" CUPCAKES		V	
SARLACC SHAKE		V	
NABOO SHEPHERD'S PIE			
SCAVENGER SCONES		V	
JEDI TEMPLE SALAD		V	
KYBER CRYSTAL CANDY	GF	V	V+

MEASUREMENT CONVERSION CHARTS

VOLUMES

US	METRIC
⅕ teaspoon (tsp)	1 ml
1 teaspoon (tsp)	5 ml
1 tablespoon (tbsp)	15 ml
1 fluid ounce (fl. oz.)	30 ml
⅕ cup	50 ml
¼ cup	60 ml
⅓ cup	80 ml
3.4 fluid ounces (fl. oz.)	100 ml
½ cup	120 ml
⅔ cup	160 ml
¾ cup	180 ml
1 cup	240 ml
1 pint (2 cups)	480 ml
1 quart (4 cups)	.95 liter

TEMPERATURES

FAHRENHEIT	CELSIUS
200°	93.3°
212°	100°
250°	120°
275°	135°
300°	150°
325°	165°
350°	177°
400°	205°
425°	220°
450°	233°
475°	245°
500°	260°

WEIGHT

US	METRIC
0.5 ounce (oz.)	14 grams (g)
1 ounce (oz.)	28 grams (g)
¼ pound (lb.)	113 grams (g)
⅓ pound (lb.)	151 grams (g)
½ pound (lb.)	227 grams (g)
1 pound (lb.)	454 grams (g)

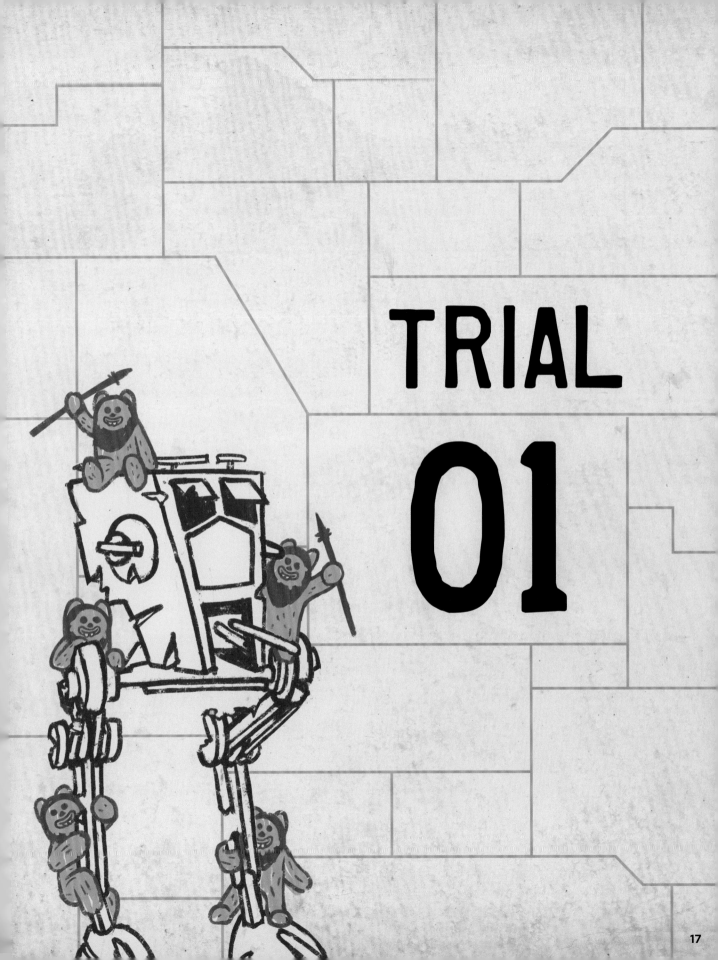

TRIAL

01

BANTHA MILK SLUSHIE

(GF, V, V+) | PREP TIME: 5 minutes (additional 24 hours)
COOKING TIME: N/A | YIELD: 1 serving

There are few things Luke Skywalker loves more than a tall glass of blue milk . . . except, perhaps, green milk, but more on that later! Sourced from banthas—the giant, hairy beasts roaming the sand dunes of Luke's home world of Tatooine—this blue milk is a staple of the young Skywalker's diet, and surely, a healthy (and refreshing!) supplement for any Padawan.

DID YOU KNOW?

Surprisingly, almonds are not true nuts. They are a type of fruit called drupes— fruit with a fleshy outer layer surrounding a shell with a seed inside, like a peach. In the case of almonds, people eat their seeds, which are delicious and packed with nutrition. Almond seeds are called "almonds" for short, and almond milk is made by grinding up almond seeds in water and filtering out any solids.

1½ cups almond milk, divided

1 tablespoon maple syrup

½ teaspoon butterfly pea flower powder

½ teaspoon vanilla extract

⅓ cup non-dairy whipped cream, for serving

1. Pour 1 cup almond milk into an ice cube tray and place in the freezer overnight.

2. Add the frozen cubes into the base of a blender. Pour in the remaining almond milk, maple syrup, butterfly pea powder, and vanilla, and blend until slushy.

3. Pour into a glass. Top with non-dairy whipped cream, to serve.

PADAWAN TRAINER SPIRALS

(V) | Prep time: 10 minutes

Cooking time: N/A | Yield: 1 serving

Between lightsaber training, lessons from Master Yoda, and exciting missions to strange, new worlds, being a Padawan learner is no easy task. That's why these Padawan Trainer Spirals are perfect for stashing away for any time that you're on the go!

1 large flour tortilla	¼ teaspoon cinnamon	1 banana, peeled
2 tablespoons peanut butter	2 tablespoons strawberry jam	

1. Onto the flour tortilla, spread the peanut butter and sprinkle with cinnamon. Spread jelly over the peanut butter.

2. Place the banana on one end. Roll up the tortilla around the banana and then use a serrated knife to cut into spirals for serving.

SNOWDRIFT SAUCE

(GF, V) | Prep time: 2 hours

Cooking time: N/A | Yield: 6 servings

When the Rebel Alliance takes shelter from the Empire on the snowy planet of Hoth, it isn't long before Luke Skywalker finds more than snowdrifts and icy caverns—the planet is, in fact, home to the carnivorous (and very hungry) wampas! This tzatziki recipe lets you recreate the snows of Hoth . . . with none of the danger, of course. Here, you will learn how to make a sauce that goes great with sliced veggies—a healthy and refreshing snack for any Padawan learner.

1 English cucumber, peeled	1 tablespoon lemon juice	½ teaspoon kosher salt
1 cup Greek yogurt	1 tablespoon chopped fresh dill	½ teaspoon black pepper
2 garlic cloves, minced	1 tablespoon chopped fresh mint	Sliced vegetables (carrots, celery, cucumbers) for serving

1. Grate the cucumber and let drain in a colander over a bowl in the refrigerator for two hours.

2. With clean hands, squeeze out the excess water from the cucumber. In a medium bowl stir together the cucumber, yogurt, garlic, lemon juice, dill, mint, salt, and pepper. Serve with vegetables.

FRUIT AND CHEESE LIGHTSABER SKEWERS

(GF, V) | Prep time: 5 minutes (additional 24 hours)
Cooking time: N/A | Yield: 1 serving

Obi-Wan Kenobi refers to lightsabers as an "elegant weapon for a more civilized age." Well, consider these picnic-ready treats an elegant snack for any hungry Padawan. Just remember that these yummy skewers are for snacking—definitely not for dueling Sith lords!

Four 1-inch pieces black tape

4 colorful plastic skewers

4 ounces cheese, cut into 8 cubes

8 grapes

8 blueberries

4 strawberries, halved

1. Take the black tape and wrap it around one end of the skewer. Set aside.

2. Skewer the cheese, grapes, blueberries, and strawberries. Serve.

DID YOU KNOW?

Cheesemaking is an ancient art. Today there are many types of cheese, from sharp cheddar to creamy Brie. Despite their differences, all cheese is made from the same basic ingredients: dairy fats and milk proteins. Cheese makers heat milk and add acid, which allows enzymes (think of them as chemical scissors) to chop the tails off certain proteins called caseins. Without these tails, milk proteins can clump together and trap fat, creating cheese curds. After cheese is made, it may be further treated by stretching, shaping, and adding microbes to preserve the cheese and enhance its flavor.

AN ICONIC SOUND EFFECT

The *vwoom* of a lightsaber blade is one of the most well-known sound effects in movie history. But how was the sound originally created? Sound designer Ben Burtt—who also designed R2-D2's beeps and Darth Vader's breathing—created the lightsaber's sounds for *Star Wars: Episode IV A New Hope* in the 1970s. Burtt was inspired by the humming of film projectors and theorized that lightsabers might make a similar noise. Searching for another aspect of the lightsaber's sound, Burtt came across a tape recorder with a broken light cable in his apartment—this provided the dangerous buzz that results from two lightsabers colliding.

OMEGA'S POPCORN MIX

(GF, V) | Prep time: 15 minutes
Cooking time: 5 minutes | Yield: 8 servings

Omega and Wrecker of the Bad Batch love to celebrate a successful mission with a bag of Mantell Mix, a snack from the planet Ord Mantell. Inspired by Omega's favorite snack, this sweet and savory popcorn mix is a great way to treat yourself for your own successes.

DID YOU KNOW?

Every kernel of popcorn is a tiny bomb, ready to explode into a delicious treat. Popcorn kernels are full of starch and water, which are tightly packed into a glassy shell called a hull. These hulls hold up well under pressure, but when popcorn is heated, the moisture in the corn turns into steam, causing pressure inside the hull to rise. At around 212° F, the rising pressure causes the hull to rupture, and the kernel explodes, inflating the popcorn starch inside into a fluffy snack.

8 cups freshly popped popcorn, divided

4 ounces purple chocolate candy melts

2 tablespoons unsalted butter, melted

2 teaspoons granulated sugar

½ teaspoon cinnamon

¼ teaspoon kosher salt

¼ cup dried raspberries

¼ cup shelled pistachios

1. Prep a baking sheet by lining it with parchment paper. Set aside.

2. Divide the popcorn in half, into two large bowls.

3. In a microwave-safe bowl, melt the chocolate candy melts for 30 seconds and then stir. Heat again for two 15 second intervals, stirring in between until melted and smooth. Toss with one of the bowls of popcorn and then spread the candy-coated popcorn onto one side of the prepped baking sheet.

4. Toss the second bowl of popcorn with the butter, sugar, cinnamon, and salt. Spread onto the other side of the baking sheet.

5. When the candy melts have set, toss the two popcorn mixes together along with the dried raspberries and pistachios. Serve.

PASAANA POPS

(GF, V) | Prep time: 3 hours
Cooking time: N/A | Yield: 6 servings

When Rey embarks on a quest to find Emperor Palpatine, she finds herself on the planet of Pasaana. The desert planet is home to the Festival of the Ancestors, a colorful celebration full of dancing and merriment that takes places once every forty-two years. With this sweet homage to the bright colors of Pasaana, you learn how to decorate delicious snacks with breakfast cereal.

DID YOU KNOW?

Bananas are members of a family of flowering tropical plants called the Musaceae (mew-zay-see-ee). Like many other fruits, they release a gas called ethene, which causes them to ripen. To make bananas ripen more quickly, store them in a brown paper bag to trap the gas. To slow ripening, store them away from other ripe fruit. Bananas are an excellent source of the minerals potassium and magnesium and contain Vitamin C. The potassium in bananas makes them slightly radioactive, but they are safe to eat.

3 large bananas, sliced in half crosswise

6 popsicle sticks

1½ cups strawberry yogurt

2 cups fruit cereal

1. Place the popsicle sticks into the bananas.

2. Dip into the yogurt, then roll into the cereal. Place on a parchment lined plate and freeze for 2 to 3 hours.

3. Let soften slightly for 2 to 3 minutes before serving.

TRIAL
02

TWIN SUNS TOAST

(V) | Prep time: 10 minutes
Cooking time: N/A | Yield: 1 serving

Rise and shine, like the twin suns of Tatooine, with this breakfast-ready toast. It is time for you to meet your destiny . . . or, you know, a school day.

1 slice whole grain bread, lightly toasted

3 tablespoons ricotta

2 teaspoons honey

2 teaspoons granola

1 small pear

2 dried apricots

1. Spread the ricotta onto the toast.

2. Use the honey and granola to create sand dune patterns.

3. Cut a 2-inch slice of pear, so you have a circular piece with one side domed. Make two cuts in the lower right corner to remove a small piece. Place flat side down onto the left side of the toast. Add a second cubed slice of pear, to create the doorway.

4. Add the two apricots as the twin suns of Tatooine.

GROGU'S AVOCADO DIP

[V] | Prep time: 15 minutes
Cooking time: N/A | Yield: 2 servings

Grogu loves nothing more than something yummy to munch on, and with this rich and creamy avocado dip, you'll have a snack that the little foundling himself would approve of.

DID YOU KNOW?

As it bakes, pita bread looks like a balloon. Pita dough, made of flour, water, salt, and yeast, is rolled into a frisbee shape and then placed in a very hot oven. As the pita bakes, the hot air causes a crust to form on the outside of the dough. Just as the water in the dough turns into steam, the flexible crust traps steam in the dough, keeping it from escaping. Pressure from the trapped steam makes the bread inflate into a giant bubble. When pita bread cools, the steam inside cools, too, allowing air to escape through small holes in the dough. A pocket remains where the steam was once trapped.

2 medium avocados, peeled and pitted

½ cup plain fat-free Greek yogurt

¼ cup cilantro, stems removed

1 garlic clove, peeled

1 tablespoon minced shallot

1 tablespoon lime juice

½ teaspoon kosher salt

¼ teaspoon onion powder

¼ teaspoon white pepper

2 kalamata olives

2 slices pink apples

2 pitas, for serving

1. Into the base of a blender add the avocados, Greek yogurt, cilantro, garlic, shallot, lime juice, salt, onion powder, and white pepper. Blend until just combined.

2. To create Grogu's head, spread the sauce into an oval shape. Add a curved triangle on both sides to make the ears. Then add a small dollop of sauce for the nose.

3. Add the kalamata olives to create the eyes, and add the pink apple for the ears. Use the back of a knife's blade to create his eyebrows by drawing one horizontal line above each of the kalamata olives. Draw four vertical lines in between the two horizontal lines, to finsh off the face details.

4. Cut the edges off of one pita to create a long trapezoid. Place this under the head to create the robe. Cut the other pita into four smaller pieces to create the overlapping scarf and the cuffs. Add small spoonfulls of the sauce on top of the cuffs to create the hands.

5. Serve the sauce with the remaining pita.

CRIMSON DAWN COOLER

[GF, V, V+] | Prep time: 10 minutes
Cooking time: N/A | Yield: 4 servings

Led by the former Sith lord Maul himself, Crimson Dawn is a criminal organization with which few in the galaxy ever dared mess around with. With its deep red color, and an orange slice that pays homage to Crimson Dawn's circular emblem, this summery beverage is criminally refreshing.

DID YOU KNOW?

Fruit is juicy because it contains lots of water. Depending on the fruit, 75 to 90 percent of its weight is made up of the molecule dihydrogen monoxide (H_2O). Plant tissue also contains gas in the spaces between cells. Up to one-fourth of an apple may be made of up of these tiny gas-filled spaces, which is why apples float in punch.

A DARK SIDE WARRIOR

Even though Maul appears to meet defeat at the hands of Obi-Wan Kenobi in *Star Wars:* Episode I *The Phantom Menace*, Maul uses the power of the dark side to stay alive. He gathers power among the criminal underworld, and he even becomes the ruler of the Mandalorians, with the fabled Darksaber by his side.

1 large orange, sliced

1 large apple, cored and cubed

2 kiwis, peeled and sliced

6 cups fruit punch

1. Add the orange, apple, and kiwis to a large pitcher. Pour in the fruit punch and refrigerate for 3 to 4 hours.
2. Pour into glasses over ice, to serve.

UNSTOPPABLE

YODA'S ILUM SNOW CHURN

(GF, V, V+) | Prep time: 4 hours
Cooking time: N/A | Yield: 2 servings

As a Jedi Master, Yoda guides Padawans to the snowy planet Ilum, where the young Jedi seek out a kyber crystal, the energy source of a lightsaber. Kyber crystals often call out to the Padawan for whom it is destined—but so too, does this frosty dessert. Find it delicious, you will.

DID YOU KNOW?

Frozen bananas are the sweetest bananas, and physics and chemistry help us understand why they taste much sweeter than fresh bananas. When bananas are frozen, water inside the banana cells turns into sharp ice crystals. These crystals destroy cell walls inside the fruit. Without these cell walls, an enzyme (chemical scissors) called amylase can access the starch in the cells, and turn it into sweet-tasting sugars.

3 very ripe bananas

3 tablespoons cocoa powder

½ teaspoon vanilla extract

1. Slice the bananas and place onto a parchment-lined baking sheet. Freeze for 2 hours, until solid.

2. In the base of a blender add the frozen bananas, cocoa powder, and vanilla. Blend until smooth like soft serve. Pour into a sealable container and freeze for another 2 hours. Scoop to serve.

TRIAL 03

HERA'S MEILOORUN SMOOTHIE

[GF, V, V+] | Prep time: 10 minutes
Cooking time: N/A | Yield: 1 serving

General Hera Syndulla is one of the greatest pilots to ever lead the Rebel Alliance, and when she's not battling Imperial squadrons, you might find her snacking on a meiloorun fruit, an orange, melon-like fruit found on the planet Lothal. This smoothie pays tribute to both that deliciously sweet fruit and the General herself.

DID YOU KNOW?

Eating mangos gives your body a big dose of vitamin C. This is important, because the human body can't produce vitamin C on its own. Also called ascorbic acid, vitamin C is a nutrient required to form blood vessels, muscles, cartilage, and a protein called collagen, which is essential for strong bones. Eating mangoes, apples, oranges, bananas, potatoes, and other fruits and vegetables is the best way to get vitamin C.

1½ cups frozen mango

½ cup non-dairy vanilla yogurt

½ cup soy milk

1 tablespoon granulated sugar

Mint, for garnish

1. Into a blender add the frozen mango, yogurt, ice, soy milk, and sugar.
2. Blend until smooth. Pour into a tall glass and add mint to serve.

MUDHORN EGG NOODLES

Prep time: 10 minutes
Cooking time: 10 minutes | Yield: 4 serving

Just as Jawas love to eat the yolk of a Mudhorn egg, you can use egg noodles to create a yummy stir fry! However, please seek a parent's permission before venturing into the cave of a Mudhorn and procuring its eggs. Or, at least, bring a Mandalorian bounty hunter with you.

DID YOU KNOW?

Most pasta is made of flour, eggs, water, and a little bit of salt. Cooking dried pasta requires heat and water, but adding water is the most important step. Dried pasta is dehydrated, which means that the water has been removed in order to keep it preserved, so that it won't mold or spoil. Adding pasta to hot water rehydrates the pasta. As it cooks, the flour starches in the pasta break down, and the proteins in the flour relax, which makes them easier to digest. Perfect pasta is cooked *al dente*, which is the sweet spot between rubbery and mushy.

1 pound beef sirloin, cut into thin strips	6 shitake mushrooms, sliced
1 tablespoon soy sauce	1 red pepper, sliced
1 tablespoon rice wine vinegar	1 cup snow peas
1 tablespoon cornstarch	2 green onions, sliced
2 packages (10 ounces) stir-fry egg noodles	8 ounces chicken broth
1 teaspoon sesame oil	¼ cup oyster sauce
1 tablespoon vegetable oil	1 teaspoon packed light brown sugar
1 garlic clove, minced	½ teaspoon kosher salt
1 teaspoon minced ginger	¼ teaspoon black pepper

1. In a medium bowl toss the beef with the soy sauce, rice vinegar, and cornstarch. Set aside.

2. Prepare the noodles according to package directions. Toss the noodles with the sesame oil. Set aside.

3. In a large skillet over medium high heat, heat the oil and cook the garlic and ginger for 1 to 2 minutes until softened and fragrant.

4. Add the meat and cook for 1 to 2 minutes, until browned. Add the mushrooms, pepper, snow peas, and onions. Cook for 2 to 3 minutes, until vegetables are softened and the meat is cooked. Add the noodles and toss to combine.

5. In a small bowl stir together the chicken broth, oyster sauce, brown sugar, salt, and pepper. Pour the sauce in the pan, tossing to coat. Cook for 1 to 2 minutes more and then serve.

JAWA SUSHI

[V] | Prep time: 30 minutes
Cooking time: 20 minutes | Yield: 10 servings

If you see a Jawa get excited, you might hear them say "Utinni!" With a plate of these yummy, Jawa-shaped sushi pockets, you might end up saying "Utinni!" yourself.

FOR THE RICE

1 cup short grain brown rice

1½ cups water

1½ tablespoons rice vinegar

1 tablespoon granulated sugar

¼ teaspoon kosher salt

FOR THE GARNISH

1 large egg

1 tablespoon olive oil

10 seasoned tofu pouches

1 sheet nori, cut into 3-by-3-inch squares

CONTINUED ON PAGE 43

DID YOU KNOW?

Here on Earth, we have thousands of varieties of rice, and all of them contain two starches: amylose and amylopectin. Depending on the ratio of these starches, rice will be soft and sticky, or firm and less sticky. Long grain rice like basmati has lots of amylose, so it is firm. Short grain rice used for sushi has mostly amylopectin, which makes it soft, sticky, and easy to sculpt.

Brown rice is brown because it still has the bran, a mineral-rich outer layer, attached. White rice has the bran removed. Converted rice is soaked and steamed to drive nutrients from the bran into the rice. Then, the rice is dried and the bran is removed.

1. Rinse the rice until water runs clear. Soak in cold water for 25 minutes and then drain.

2. In a large pot, add the rice and water. Bring to a boil. Cover and reduce heat and then simmer for 20 minutes until the water is absorbed. Remove from heat and let sit for 10 minutes, covered.

3. Transfer the rice into a large bowl and fold in the rice vinegar, sugar, and salt. Let cool slightly.

4. In a small bowl, use a fork to scramble the egg. In a small pan over medium heat, add the oil and pour in the egg. When the bottom has set, fold the edges over to form an omelet. Remove from pan and set aside.

5. Carefully pull open the tofu pouch. Stuff with 3 to 4 tablespoons of rice. Place a piece of nori on the outside.

6. Use a tiny round cutter to cut out circles from the omelet and then place on the nori to form the eyes. Repeat with the remaining tofu pouches and rice.

ANAKIN'S BOONTA EVE COB

(GF, V) | Prep time: 10 minutes
Cooking time: 40 minutes | Yield: 4 servings

If you've ever seen a podrace, you know how dangerous it can be. In fact, it's so dangerous, that no humans have ever competed, let alone won. Anakin Skywalker is the notable outlier, and his strength with the Force, plus a knack for all-things machinery, gives him the edge to not only survive a podrace, but win one of the greatest, the Boonta Eve Classic. As a snack that one might find at the podracing arena, this Boonta Eve Cob celebrates Anakin's amazing victory.

DID YOU KNOW?

When cooking raw sweet corn on the cob, there are two major players—starches and pectin. Pectin is a biological glue that holds plant cells together. As raw corn cooks, pectin in the cell walls dissolves, and the corn gets softer. Heat and water absorption causes raw, chalky white starches inside the kernels to become smooth and transparent.

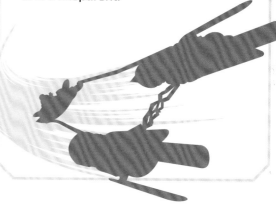

4 ears corn, in husk

2 tablespoons unsalted butter, melted

¼ cup mayonnaise

½ cup cotija cheese, crumbled

1 teaspoon chili powder

½ teaspoon garlic salt

¼ cup crema

2 tablespoons minced cilantro

1. Preheat the oven to 375ºF. Place the corn directly on the oven rack. Cook for 40 minutes. Let cool slightly for 2 to 3 minutes.

2. Pull back the husks. Brush with melted butter, then brush on the mayonnaise.

3. Roll the cob in the cotija cheese. Sprinkle with the chili powder and garlic salt. Drizzle the crema over the corn. Sprinkle with the cilantro before serving.

DARTH VADER'S MUSTAFAR FRUIT CUPS

(GF, V) | Prep time: 10 minutes

Cooking time: N/A | Yield: 4 servings

The dark, blood-red colors of this spiced, zesty snack are an homage to Darth Vader and the planet that he calls home during his time as a Sith lord, Mustafar. A coat of chili powder tops off fresh fruit, adding a touch of spice.

1 tablespoon chili powder

2 teaspoons lime zest, divided

¼ teaspoon kosher salt

⅛ teaspoon packed light brown sugar

1 cup raspberries

1 cup strawberries, hulled and quartered

1 cup blueberries

1 cup blackberries

1 lime, quartered

DID YOU KNOW?

Chili peppers taste "hot" due to a family of chemical compounds called capsaicinoids (cap-say-sin-oids). When you eat chili peppers or chili powder, these chemicals bind to a structure in your mouth called a receptor, like a key into a lock. This particular receptor senses high temperatures and sends a signal to your brain that you've eaten something hot, producing a burning sensation.

A SITH LORD'S HOME

Darth Vader dwells on the dark side of the Force, from within the walls of his castle, which rises above the fiery landscape of Mustafar. Within his castle, Vader spends much time inside a bacta tank—a chamber full of healing fluid, which Vader needs to provide ongoing treatment of his wounds. During these times, he meditates, drawing strength from the dark side.

1. In a small bowl stir together the chili powder, 1 teaspoon of the lime zest, salt, and brown sugar. Set aside.

2. Into four parfait glasses add ¼ cup of raspberries. Top with ¼ cup of blackberries. Sprinkle ⅛ teaspoon of the chili powder mixture over the berries.

3. Add ¼ cup of strawberries and then ¼ cup of blueberries. Sprinkle ¼ teaspoon of the chili powder mixture over the top. Sprinkle ¼ teaspoon of lime zest on top. Serve with a lime wedge.

TRIAL

04

ASTROMECH DROID

CHOPPER CHEESE TOAST

Prep time: 15 minutes

Cooking time: 2 minutes | Yield: 1 serving

Now this is the droid you're looking for! These grilled cheese sandwiches are stacked to look like Chopper, the loyal (but cranky) droid who is never too far from the rebel hero Hera Syndulla.

DID YOU KNOW?

A chemical reaction called the Maillard reaction is responsible for the unique, delicious flavor in foods like grilled cheese and seared steak. This mouth-watering process occurs when certain sugars and proteins are exposed to dry heat. As a grilled cheese sandwich is heated up, milk proteins and fat in butter, along with starchy sugars and wheat proteins in bread, break down and recombine, forming thousands of new chemical compounds that create a toasty flavor profile.

2 slices white bread

2 slices white cheddar cheese

2 slices American cheese

1 slice ham

CONTINUED ON PAGE 51

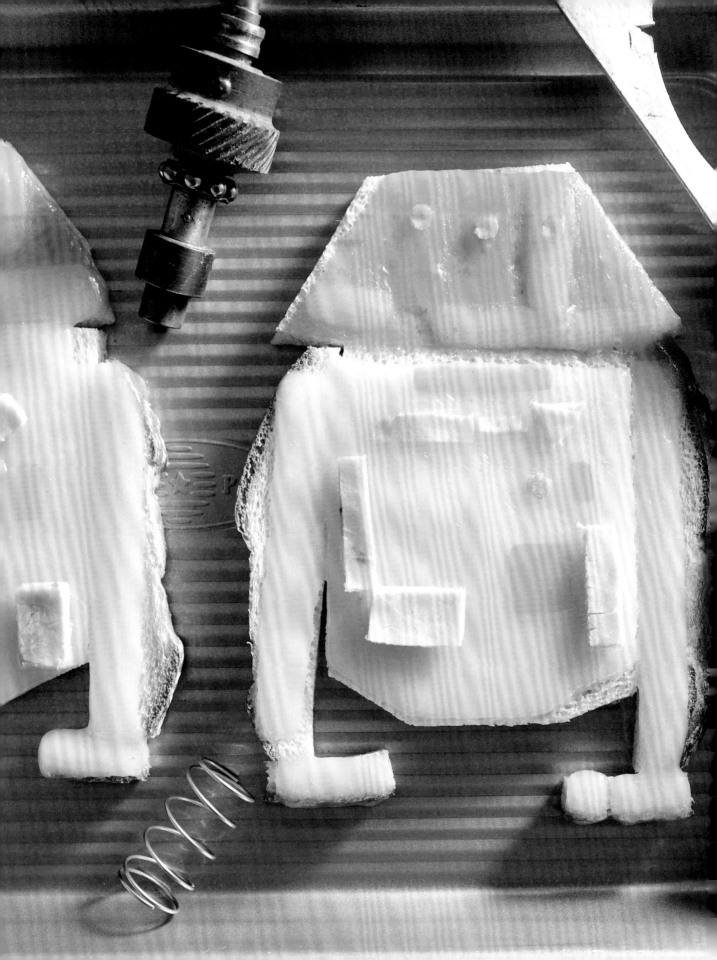

1. Cut the crusts off one piece of bread, creating a 6-by-5-inch square. Place onto a quarter baking sheet lined with parchment paper. Place a piece of white cheddar on top. Set aside.

2. Cut the second slice of bread into a trapezoid with a 5-inch base and that is 3 inches tall. Position this above the square piece of bread. Cut a piece of American cheese to fit and place on the trapezoid.

3. Use the bread scraps to create Chopper's legs. These should look like an "L."

4. Cut pieces of cheese and ham to create Chopper's details.

5. Place the baking sheet into a toaster oven and lightly toast for 1 to 2 minutes until the cheese has melted.

SITH SOUPERS

[GF, V, V+] | Prep time: 30 minutes
Cooking time: 45 minutes | Yield: 8 servings

When Emperor Palpatine returns to destroy Rey and the Resistance once and for all, his army of Sith devotees rises to serve his dark bidding. Palpatine's army includes legions of Sith troopers, all clad in fearsome red armor. Though the Sith troopers were meant to strike fear into the heart of the galaxy, this tomato soup is thankfully far less intimidating.

1 tablespoon olive oil

1 large sweet onion, diced

2 garlic cloves, minced

1 tablespoon tomato paste

8 ounces vegetable stock

1 can (8 ounces) tomato sauce

2 cans (28 ounces) diced tomatoes

2 tablespoons granulated sugar

1 tablespoon basil

1 tablespoon oregano

1 tablespoon parsley

2 teaspoons kosher salt

½ teaspoon black pepper

Blue corn tortilla chips, round

1. In a Dutch oven over medium heat, add the olive oil and onions. Cook for 5 minutes, until the onions have softened.

2. Add the garlic and cook for 1 minute, until fragrant. Stir in the tomato paste and cook for 1 minute more.

3. Pour in the vegetable stock, tomato sauce, diced tomatoes, sugar, basil, oregano, parsley, salt, and pepper. Bring to a boil and then reduce heat to low. Simmer for 45 minutes.

4. Use an immersion blender and puree until smooth.

5. Ladle soup into bowls. Create the Sith trooper's eyes by breaking a tortilla chip into two semicircles. Crush additional tortilla chips, and use them to create the Sith trooper helmet details.

MOOF MILK PARFAIT

(GF, V) | Prep time: 10 minutes
Cooking time: N/A | Yield: 4 servings

When Han Solo finds himself in the *Millennium Falcon*, after years of it belonging to the vile Unkar Plutt, he is dismayed that Plutt dared to mess around with the fastest ship in the galaxy! But what is moof milk exactly? As its name suggests, this substance comes from an animal called a moof, and it is used in the *Star Wars* galaxy to make yogurt. Even though calling someone a "moof-milker" might not be the nicest thing you can do, giving someone a glass of this Moof Milk Parfait would have the opposite effect.

> " *Hey! Some moof-milker installed a compressor on the ignition line!* "
>
> **—Han Solo**

DID YOU KNOW?

Eating certain beneficial microbes, like the ones in yogurt, can be good for your gut. Billions of creatures too small to see without a microscope (microorganisms) live in your intestinal tract and are collectively known as your microbiome. The balance of different types of bacteria that live there can have a huge impact on your health. Eating fermented food such as yogurt can help to introduce "good" bacteria to the microbe mixture in your gut. Besides helping with digestion, beneficial bacteria crowd out other microbes called pathogens that can make you sick.

1 cup strawberries, hulled and quartered	2 kiwis, peeled and cubed
16 ounces vanilla yogurt	¼ cup granola
1 cup mango chunks	1 tablespoon shredded coconut

1. Into four parfait glasses, add ¼ cup strawberries. Top with 2 tablespoons of yogurt.

2. Add a layer of ¼ cup of mango. Top with another 2 tablespoons of yogurt.

3. Add ¼ cup of kiwi and a dollop of yogurt.

4. Sprinkle the granola and coconut on top and serve.

GINGER "SNAP" WEXLEYS

[V] | Prep time: 30 minutes
Cooking time: 8 minutes | Yield: 30 cookies

Snap Wexley is one of the most skilled pilots in the Resistance fleet, and we often see him valiantly flying alongside Poe Dameron. These gingersnaps are a fitting tribute to one of the finest heroes of the Resistance.

FOR THE COOKIES

2 cups all-purpose flour

1½ teaspoons baking soda

2 teaspoons ground ginger

2 teaspoons cinnamon

½ teaspoon cloves

¼ teaspoon kosher salt

¾ cup vegetable shortening

1 cup granulated sugar

1 large egg

¼ cup molasses

⅓ cup granulated sugar, for rolling

FOR THE ICING

2 cups confectioners' sugar

1 to 2 tablespoons whole milk

2 teaspoons light corn syrup

½ teaspoon clear vanilla extract

⅛ teaspoon kosher salt

Orange food coloring

1. In a large bowl whisk together the flour, baking soda, ginger, cinnamon, cloves, and salt. Set aside.

2. In the bowl of an electric mixer, cream the shortening and sugar for 2 to 3 minutes, until fluffy. Stir in the egg and molasses.

3. Add the flour mixture, just until the dough comes together. Refrigerate for 20 minutes.

4. Preheat the oven to 350ºF. Prep baking sheets with parchment.

5. Use a small scoop to make 1-inch balls. Roll in the granulated sugar and place onto the prepped baking sheets. Bake for 10 minutes.

6. Let cool on the pan for 2 minutes and then move to a wire rack to cool.

7. In a small bowl whisk together confectioners' sugar, milk, corn syrup, clear vanilla, and salt. Whisk until smooth.

8. Remove two-thirds of the icing into a separate small bowl. Whisk in the orange food coloring, until combined. If the icing is too thick, add more milk one teaspoon at a time, if needed.

9. Dip the cookies into the orange icing. Let set for 10 minutes, then drizzle the white icing down the center, to recreate the colors of a Rebel flight suit.

10. When the icing has set, the cookies are ready to serve.

RED FIVE'S REFRESHMENT

(GF, V, V+) | Prep time: 10 minutes
Cooking time: N/A | Yield: 6 servings

When Luke Skywalker piloted an X-wing in the Rebel Alliance's attack on the first Death Star, he flew under the title Red Five, as a member of a team of starfighters called Red Squadron. Destroying a Death Star is no small task, and Luke might've enjoyed a refreshing beverage like this one, just before accepting the Medal of Bravery from Princess Leia.

DID YOU KNOW?

Seeds or no seeds? Like humans, watermelon plants evolved to have two sets of chromosomes. Chromosomes are packages of DNA (deoxyribonucleic acid) containing all the information needed for life. More than 50 years ago, a Japanese scientist figured out how to grow watermelons that contained three sets of chromosomes, instead of the normal two sets. Because they had three sets of chromosomes, the watermelons were unable to produce normal seeds. The seedless watermelon was born!

3 cups cubed watermelon

½ cup fresh lemon juice

½ cup granulated sugar

3 cups cold water

6 slices watermelon, cut into Rebel symbol

1. Into a blender add the cubed watermelon, lemon juice, and sugar. Blend until smooth. Add the water and blend until combined.

2. Pour over ice to serve. Garnish with the watermelon symbols.

TRIAL

05

R2-KT RICE BALLS

[GF] | Prep time: 45 minutes
Cooking time: 15 minutes | Yield: 6 servings

R2-KT is a pink droid with a heart of gold! When a young fan named Katie was diagnosed with cancer, the R2-D2 Builders Club created a pink droid to keep her company. Onscreen, we see R2-KT stand against the Galactic Empire and the First Order, but in the real world, the brave droid spreads awareness of pediatric illness, makes visits to children's hospitals, and fundraises for charities. As a salute to R2-KT, these rice balls are as yummy as she is courageous.

FOR THE RICE
2 cups short grain rice

2½ cups water

½ teaspoon kosher salt

FOR THE DECORATION
5 to 6 slices ham

1 sheet nori

1. Rinse the rice until water runs clear. Soak in cold water for 25 minutes and then drain.

2. In a large pot add the rice and water. Bring to a boil. Cover and reduce heat and then simmer for 15 minutes until the water is absorbed. Remove from heat and let sit for 10 minutes, covered.

3. Transfer the rice into a large bowl and fold in the salt.

4. Line a 4-ounce bowl with plastic wrap. Scoop the rice into the bowl and press down. Turn the bowl over and release onto a plate. Repeat with the rest of the rice.

5. Cut the ham and nori into pieces to decorate the rice balls. Use the ham to create the colored plates of the droid and use the nori to create the droid's eye. Serve immediately.

BLURRG FEED

[V] | Prep time: 5 minutes
Cooking time: 20 minutes | Yield: 4 servings

Blurrgs may not be the most intelligent creatures, but they're incredibly useful for agriculture. Farmers, for instance, are known to use blurrgs to clear patches of weeds, since they feed on grass. This dish recreates a typical blurrg's greens-based diet, adding crumbly Parmesan cheese and farro, a satisfying grain.

DID YOU KNOW?

Cereals are the seeds of grasses, including wheat, rice, and corn. The grains of cereal can be separated into three different parts: the bran, the germ, and the endosperm. The bran is the bulky outer layer, which contains vitamins and minerals. The germ lies inside the bran and contains fat, which can cause grain to spoil. The endosperm is the main part of a cereal grain and is made mostly of starch and protein. Farro is a certain type of wheat with the bran and the germ removed.

2 cups vegetable broth

1 cup farro

2 cups fresh spinach leaves

½ teaspoon kosher salt

¼ teaspoon black pepper

⅓ cup grated Parmesan cheese

1. In a large saucepan stir together vegetable broth and farro. Bring to a boil. Reduce heat and simmer for 20 minutes, until the broth has been absorbed.

2. Stir in the spinach, salt, and pepper.

3. Sprinkle with Parmesan and serve.

ENDOR ROLLS

[GF] | Prep time: 15 minutes
Cooking time: N/A | Yield: 8 rolls

The Forest Moon of Endor is lush with all sorts of flora and fauna, and this no-cook roll would be right at home in an Ewok feast.

2 ounces rice vermicelli noodles

8 spring roll rice wrappers

16 medium cooked shrimp, peeled and deveined

¼ cup fresh cilantro

1 medium carrot, peeled and cut into matchsticks

1 small cucumber, thinly sliced

¼ cup fresh mint leaves

Sweet chili sauce, for serving

DID YOU KNOW?

Rice paper contains lots of starch, which makes it brittle. Starchy as rice paper may be, the starch is called a gelling agent. This means that when you add liquid to rice paper, the rice paper transforms into a soft, flexible gel that you can almost see through. Rice paper also contains fibers called cellulose, which are edible but don't dissolve in water. Because cellulose doesn't dissolve, these fibers help hold rice paper together.

1. In a large bowl, add the rice vermicelli noodles. Pour over boiling water, completely covering the noodles. Soak for 2 to 3 minutes, until softened. Drain and set aside.

2. Pour warm water into a pie pan. Place one rice wrapper into the water and let soak for just 15 seconds, until pliable. Move to a clean surface.

3. Place two shrimp into the center of the rice paper. Top with the cilantro, carrot, cucumber, rice vermicelli noodles, and mint. Fold over the bottom of the rice paper, then the sides, and roll tightly.

4. Repeat with the remaining rice paper and ingredients. Serve with sweet chili sauce.

TAKODANA SALAD

(GF, V, V+) | Prep time: 10 minutes
Cooking time: 30 minutes | Yield: 6 servings

When Rey first spots Takodana's abundant wildlife from inside the *Millennium Falcon*, she remarks, "I didn't know there was this much green in the whole galaxy." This vibrant, colorful salad is a wonderfully nutritious nod to the planet's lush forests!

1 cup broccoli florets

1 cup cauliflower florets

1 cup cherry tomatoes

8 ounces mushrooms, halved

1 medium zucchini, cut into chunks

1 bell pepper, seeded and cut into chunks

1 red onion, peeled and cut into chunks

2 cloves garlic

⅓ cup olive oil

1 tablespoon oregano

1 teaspoon basil

½ teaspoon kosher salt

¼ teaspoon black pepper

1½ tablespoons balsamic vinegar

1 tablespoon lemon juice

DID YOU KNOW?

Sugars are sweet-tasting carbohydrates found in living tissues. Many plants and vegetables contain different types of sugars called glucose, sucrose, and fructose. Roasting vegetables causes the sugars inside to release a range of complex, delicious flavors. Roasting is also a good way to retain nutrients in vegetables, because no water is involved in the process—that way, water can't leech away the nutrients.

A WELL-TRAVELED CHEF

Takodana is home to Maz Kanata, a pirate, whose castle attracts all sorts of smugglers and outlaws. A chef named Strono "Cookie" Tuggs runs Maz's kitchen, but when the First Order destroys the castle, Cookie is left to roam the galaxy. That is, until he lands his ship on Batuu, a planet on the galaxy's edge. At Batuu's Black Spire Outpost, Cookie sells delicious meals to any who come to visit the outpost's many attractions.

1. Preheat oven to 400ºF. Prep baking sheet with parchment paper.

2. In a large bowl toss the broccoli, cauliflower, cherry tomatoes, mushrooms, zucchini, bell pepper, red onion, garlic, olive oil, oregano, basil, salt, and pepper.

3. Spread on baking sheet and cook for 30 minutes until softened, and slightly charred.

4. Drizzle with balsamic vinegar and lemon juice. Serve.

BUTTER CHEWIES

[GF, V] | Prep time: 20 minutes
Cooking time: 1 hour | Yield: 12 servings

Chewbacca likes to think with his stomach, and sometimes it lands him and Han Solo in trouble. But, can you blame him? We're all a little food-motivated, at times. When was the last time you treated yourself with a special snack after a tiring day at school? Next time, try preparing a plate of coconut-topped butter mochi. These mini versions of Chewie are nutty, rich, and well . . . chewy!

DID YOU KNOW?

Coconut milk is the white liquid squeezed from grated coconut and used for cooking and baking. It can be creamy or thin, depending on how much fat it contains. Coconut milk will be thin if there is little fat and thick if there is a lot of fat.

FOR THE MOCHI

16 ounces mochiko

2½ cups granulated sugar

1½ teaspoons baking powder

¼ teaspoon kosher salt

1 can (14 ounces) coconut milk

1 can (12 ounces) evaporated milk

½ cup (1 stick) unsalted butter, melted

4 large eggs, beaten slightly

2 teaspoons vanilla extract

FOR THE TOPPING

1½ cups shredded coconut

2 tablespoons granulated sugar

½ teaspoon cinnamon

FOR THE DECORATION

4 ounces chocolate candy melts

2 ounces black candy melts

2 ounces white candy melts

CONTINUED ON PAGE 69

1. Preheat the oven to 350°F. Prep a 13-by-9 inch pan with parchment paper and non-stick spray.

2. In a large bowl whisk together the mochiko, sugar, baking powder, and salt. Make a well in the center of the dry ingredients and stir in the coconut milk, evaporated milk, butter, eggs, and vanilla. Pour into the prepped pan.

3. In a small bowl mix together the coconut, sugar, and cinnamon. Sprinkle over the batter. Bake for 1 hour, until set.

4. Let cool completely. Use a plastic knife to cut into twelve rectangles.

5. In a microwave-safe bowl, melt the chocolate candy melts for 30 seconds, then stir. Heat again for two 15 second intervals, stirring in between until melted and smooth. Pour into a piping bag. Set aside. Do the same for the black and white candy melts.

6. Use the chocolate candy melts to pipe a bandolier in a diagonal across the mochi. Then pipe the black icing to create the Wookiee's eyes and nose.

7. Finally, use the candy melts to create the teeth and bandolier details.

8. Once the candy melts have set, the mochi is ready to serve.

TRIAL

06

MAUL CAKES

[V, V+] | Prep time: 10 minutes
Cooking time: 10 minutes | Yield: 1 serving

There's no doubt that Darth Maul is one of the most fearsome warriors in the galaxy. This pancake mimics the Sith lord's scowling visage and is filled with kimchi, which gives it a fiery hue worthy of Maul's raging temperament.

Beware of the dark side

½ cup all-purpose flour

½ cup mochiko

½ cup soy milk

1 tablespoon gochujang

1 cup chopped kimchi

1 green onion, minced

1 tablespoon vegetable oil

FOR THE GARNISH

3 to 4 tablespoons black sesame seeds

1 small white onion

½ teaspoon Sriracha hot sauce

1. In a large bowl, whisk together the flour and mochiko. Make a well in the center and stir in the soy milk and gochujang. Fold in the kimchi and green onions.

2. In a large skillet over medium heat, add oil and pour the batter into the pan, spreading to flatten into a large pancake.

3. Cook for 3 to 4 minutes, until lightly browned. Flip over and cook for another 2 to 3 minutes, until cooked through.

4. Move the pancake to a serving plate. Use the black sesame seeds to create Maul's face pattern.

5. Slice the onions to create his horns, eyes, and teeth. Add the Sriracha and two black sesame seeds for the pupils. Serve immediately.

MON CALA PARCELS

(GF) | Prep time: 10 minutes
Cooking time: 15 minutes | Yield: 4 servings

Mon Calamari like Admiral Ackbar are amphibious, meaning they can live on land or in water. This savory baked seafood dish would be a hit on their home planet of Mon Cala.

Four 6-ounce salmon fillets

¼ cup sliced shallot

2 tablespoons unsalted butter, cubed

½ teaspoon kosher salt

¼ teaspoon black pepper

12 lemon slices

4 sprigs fresh thyme

DID YOU KNOW?

"En papillote" means "in paper" in French. Fish en papillote is fish wrapped in parchment paper or foil envelopes, with a little bit of liquid inside. The packets of fish are placed in the oven and heated so that the liquid boils and evaporates to form steam. The steam carries energy in the form of heat to the fish and cooks it by denaturing (unraveling) the proteins inside. As it cooks, fish turns from translucent (see-through) to opaque (white or pink), much like an egg white.

A HEROIC LEGACY

Admiral Ackbar is one of the greatest heroes of the Rebel Alliance, and he goes on to fight the First Order, as a leader of the Resistance. Later, his son, Aftab, follows suit, fighting as a Resistance colonel and helping to defeat Emperor Palpatine once and for all at the Battle of Exegol.

1. Preheat the oven to 400°F.

2. Place a salmon filet onto a piece of parchment paper. Top with shallots, butter, salt, and pepper. Add three lemon slices, and a sprig of thyme. Repeat with the other three filets.

3. Fold over and crimp the edges of the paper to close.

4. Place the packets onto a baking sheet and bake for 10 to 15 minutes, until cooked through.

5. Cut open parchment and serve.

BATUUAN GARLIC GRAINS

(GF, V, V+) | Prep time: 5 minutes
Cooking time: 10 minutes | Yield: 8 servings

The Outer Rim planet Batuu isn't just home to the bustling Black Spire Outpost—it also boasts a variety of different types of native grains, much like the kind used in this wholesome rice dish. Next time you're stopping by Dok-Ondar's Den of Antiquities or Oga's Cantina, bring this along as a meal that the locals might enjoy!

2 tablespoons olive oil

14 garlic cloves, minced

4 cups cooked white rice

¼ teaspoon kosher salt

¼ teaspoon black pepper

2 green onions, minced

1. In a large skillet over medium heat, add the olive oil and garlic. Cook for 3 to 4 minutes until lightly browned. Scoop out the garlic and set aside, leaving the oil.

2. Add the rice to the oil and cook for 3 to 4 minutes, until softened.

3. Reserve 1 tablespoon of the garlic, and stir the rest into the rice.

4. Season with salt and pepper. Garnish with remaining garlic and green onions, to serve.

AHSOKA'S JELLY CUBES

(GF) | Prep time: 24 hours to set
Cooking time: N/A | Yield: 12 servings

Once the Padawan of Anakin Skywalker, Ahsoka Tano leaves the Jedi Order to find her own path, eventually serving as one of the founding members of the Rebel Alliance. The bright blue, orange, and white colors of this sweet jelly are a stunning homage to Ahsoka Tano, one of the bravest, most independent heroes that the galaxy has ever seen.

DID YOU KNOW?

Contrary to what its name might suggest, condensed milk cannot be made by putting cartons of milk in the Death Star's trash compactor! Instead, it is made through the process of evaporation. Milk is mostly made of water, and heating milk adds lots of energy to the liquid, causing water vapor (a gas) to form. When most of the water has evaporated, a thick substance called evaporated milk remains. To sweeten the milk, lots of sugar is added. The high sugar content also prevents the growth of harmful microbes. The sweetened, evaporated milk is then canned. The resulting liquid is a high-viscosity (thick) suspension of milk proteins, fats, and sugars—aka condensed milk—which is used in delicious recipes all across planet Earth.

FOR THE ORANGE GELATIN

6 ounces orange gelatin

2 cups boiling water

FOR THE BLUE GELATIN

6 ounces blue raspberry gelatin

2 cups boiling water

FOR THE WHITE GELATIN

2 envelopes unflavored gelatin

2 cups boiling water

1 can (14 ounces) sweetened condensed milk

CONTINUED ON NEXT PAGE

1. In a medium bowl, dissolve the orange gelatin into the boiling water. Whisk until clear. Pour into a small container, and cover. Set aside.

2. In a separate medium bowl, dissolve the blue raspberry gelatin into the boiling water. Whisk until clear. Pour into a separate small container, and cover.

3. Refrigerate both gelatins for 5 hours, or until solid.

4. When solid, cut gelatin into cubes and lightly toss together in a 13-by-9-inch pan. Set aside.

5. In a medium bowl, dissolve the unflavored gelatin in the boiling water. Let cool slightly and then whisk in the sweetened condensed milk, until smooth. Let cool for 15 minutes.

6. When cooled, gently pour over the orange and blue gelatin cubes. Cover with plastic wrap and refrigerate overnight.

7. Cut into squares, to serve.

BESPIN BREW

(GF, V) | Prep time: 15 minutes
Cooking time: N/A | Yield: 4 servings

On their way to Cloud City, Han Solo, Leia Organa, and Chewbacca make their way through the pink-tinged skies of the planet Bespin. The bright hue of this creamy strawberry beverage celebrates the planet's colorful atmosphere.

DID YOU KNOW?

Starch is a complex carbohydrate: a long chain of carbon, hydrogen, and oxygen atoms. Most plants, such as rice, wheat, and potatoes, store their energy as starch. Because it is a white solid at room temperature and doesn't dissolve in water, starches such as rice make a good thickener for drinks and sauces.

---

1 cup uncooked white long-grain rice

5 cups water

16 ounces strawberries, hulled

4 cinnamon sticks

1 can (12 ounces) evaporated milk

½ cup granulated sugar

1 teaspoon vanilla extract

Cinnamon sticks, for garnish

Strawberries, for garnish

---

1. Into a blender, add the rice, water, and strawberries. Blend until the rice is finely ground, 2 to 3 minutes. Pour the mixture into a large bowl along with cinnamon sticks. Soak overnight in the refrigerator.

2. Sieve the rice water into a serving pitcher; discarding the rice and cinnamon sticks.

3. Stir in the evaporated milk, sugar, and vanilla, stirring until combined and the sugar has dissolved. Refrigerate until ready to serve.

4. Pour over ice and garnish with cinnamon sticks and strawberries for serving.

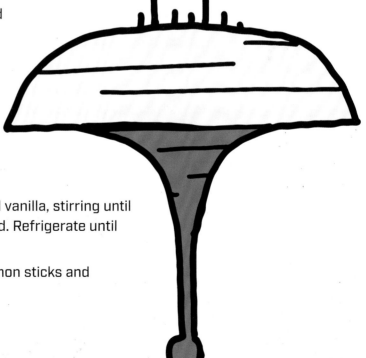

LUKE SKYWALKER'S AHCH-TO SMOOTHIE

(GF, V, V+) | Prep time: 10 minutes
Cooking time: N/A | Yield: 1 serving

After exiling himself to Ahch-To, the birthplace of the Jedi Order, a disillusioned Luke Skywalker spends his days living as a hermit and harvesting green milk from marine mammals called thala-sirens. This creamy, green concoction is the ideal refreshment for Jedi Masters and Padawans alike—hopefully, you'll feel a little less grumpy than Luke does after taking a sip!

DID YOU KNOW?

There's more to blending food than meets the eye. Blades play a large role in chopping up food, but once the pieces get small enough, the blades can't do much more. That's when powerful hydrodynamic forces come into play. The shearing force of the blender blades creates a powerful, tornado-like vortex in the blender that sucks liquid down and flings it against the side of the blender. Turbulence rips small pieces of food apart, and bubbles form in the fluid, causing violent shock waves when they collapse. All this helps break down the smaller pieces of food, resulting in a delicious smoothie!

LUKE'S FELLOW ISLANDERS

Luke Skywalker shares Ahch-To with plenty of creatures, including bird-like animals called porgs. The porgs were created by the filmmakers of *Star Wars: Episode VIII The Last Jedi* as a nod to the puffins that inhabit the island of Skellig Michael, the location that stood in for Ahch-To during filming.

1 banana, sliced and frozen

1 small avocado, peeled and pitted

1 cup soy milk

2 tablespoons maple syrup

½ teaspoon vanilla

⅛ teaspoon cinnamon

1. Into a blender, add the frozen banana, avocado, soy milk, maple syrup, and vanilla. Blend until smooth.

2. Pour into a glass. Dust the edge with cinnamon and serve.

TRIAL

07

PASTRY PUFFER PIGS

Prep time: 20 minutes

Cooking time: 15 minutes | Yield: 5 servings

Puffer pigs are important tools for the galaxy's miners, since these creatures can sniff out valuable minerals. Ever the fortune seeker, Lando Calrissian himself once owned a puffer pig! After baking this warm, doughy dish, you'll enjoy sniffing out the rich ham and cheese filling inside.

1 egg plus 1 tablespoon water, for egg wash

2 rolls pre-made pie dough

5 slices cheddar cheese

5 slices ham

5 peppercorns

½ teaspoon cumin

½ teaspoon onion powder

½ teaspoon kosher salt

1. Preheat the oven to 400ºF. Prep a baking sheet with parchment paper.

2. In a small bowl, whisk the egg and water to make the egg wash. Set aside.

3. Roll out the dough and cut into ten 5-by-3-inch rectangles. On one of the dough rectangles, place a slice of cheese and a slice of ham, folding over if necessary.

4. Brush the edges with the egg wash, then top with a second dough rectangle. Press the edges to seal. Trim the edges of the dough to create rounded edges. Use the excess dough to add spiny details along the top, as well as a tail, nose, and eyes. Brush with egg wash. Place a peppercorn for the eye.

5. In a small bowl, stir together the cumin, onion powder, and salt. Sprinkle a small amount along the top spiny edge of the pie. Place onto the baking sheet. Repeat with the rest of the dough to create five hand pies in total.

6. Bake for 15 minutes, until golden brown. Let cool for 5 minutes, before serving.

NERF NUGGETS

Prep time: 10 minutes

Cooking time: 15 minutes| Yield: 4 servings

Nerf meat is a delicacy across the galaxy, served in dishes like soups and steaks—or, in this case, sweet and salty meatballs that are perfect for either a quick dinner or school lunch the next day!

DID YOU KNOW?

When cooking with ground meat, remember that everything that was on the outside of the piece of meat before it was ground will now be in the middle of every burger or meatball—and that includes harmful bacteria. That's why ground meat should always be cooked to a temperature that will kill these types of bacteria. For example, *Campylobacter* (cam-pie-lo-back-ter) and Salmonella (sam-oh-nell-uh) bacteria are sometimes found on chicken, but can be killed by cooking the meat to 165° F. Using a meat thermometer is a quick and easy way to check the temperature at the center of a meatball or burger.

FOR THE SAUCE

¼ cup soy sauce

2 tablespoons mirin (sweet rice wine)

2 teaspoons packed light brown sugar

1 teaspoon lemon juice

FOR THE CHICKEN

1½ pounds ground chicken

¼ cup panko breadcrumbs

2 green onions, minced

1 garlic clove, minced

1 teaspoon minced ginger

1 tablespoon cornstarch

1 tablespoon soy sauce

2 teaspoons mirin

1 teaspoon sesame oil

¼ teaspoon white pepper

1 large egg

ADDITIONAL SUPPLIES

Eight 6-inch wooden skewers

1. Soak wooden skewers in a shallow pan of water. Set aside.

2. In a small bowl whisk the soy sauce, mirin, brown sugar, and lemon juice. Set aside.

3. In a large bowl, combine ground chicken, panko, green onions, garlic, ginger, cornstarch, soy sauce, mirin, sesame oil, white pepper, and egg. Form mixture into cubes and place onto the wooden skewers.

4. In a large skillet over medium high heat, add the skewered chicken and cook for 5 minutes, until browned. Flip the skewers over, cover and cook for another 10 minutes, until cooked through.

5. Brush on the sauce, then cook for another 30 seconds. Serve immediately.

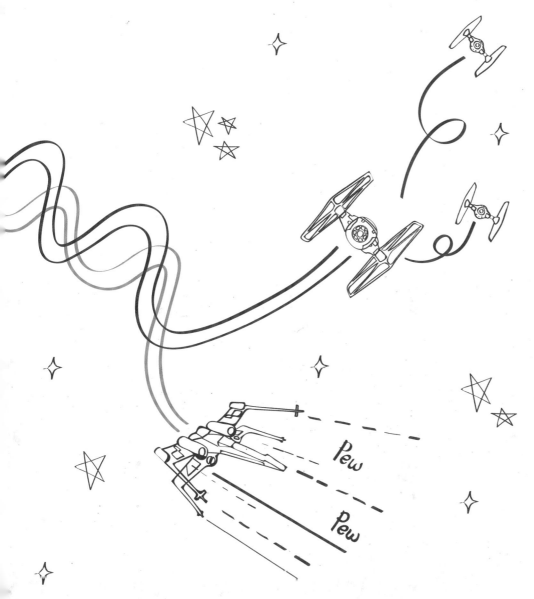

JOGAN FRUIT PUFFS

(V) | Prep time: 10 minutes
Cooking time: 20 minutes | Yield: 9 servings

Jogan fruit, a bright purple plant that grows on the planet Lothal, is a healthy snack for any Jedi on the go. Here, it's baked into a scrumptious dessert that you can savor after a long day of training.

DID YOU KNOW?

Gelatin is made up of a suspension of tiny particles in a water-based solution, called a semi-solid hydrocolloid (high-dro-coll-oid). When gelatin is dissolved in hot water, the proteins inside them move around more easily, and the gelatin looks like a liquid. When the solution cools down, the proteins lose energy, stop moving, and stick together, trapping pockets of water, and creating a gel.

---

1 package (17 ounces) puff pastry, thawed

½ cup cream cheese, softened

½ cup blackberry jam

1 large egg plus 1 tablespoon water, for egg wash

¼ cup confectioners' sugar

---

1. Preheat the oven to 400° F. Prep a baking sheet with parchment paper.

2. Cut one sheet of puff pastry into nine equal pieces. Add a tablespoon of cream cheese in the center of a square and top with one tablespoon of jam.

3. Cut the second piece of puff pastry into nine equal pieces. Place a piece on top of a cream cheese topped square, pressing the edges to close. Lightly score the top with a knife. Repeat for remaining 8 pastries.

4. Bake for 18 minutes, until golden brown. Dust with confectioners' sugar prior to serving.

STORMTROOPER DONUTS

[V] | Prep time: 10 minutes
Cooking time: 15 minutes | Yield: 12 donuts

Commanded by the likes of Darth Vader, Emperor Palpatine, and Kylo Ren, stormtroopers are stationed across the galaxy to enforce tyranny. Luckily, when it comes to this army of sweet donuts, the only agenda they'll be enforcing is that of a tasty treat!

FOR THE DONUTS

1½ cups all-purpose flour

¼ cup granulated sugar

2 teaspoons baking powder

¼ teaspoon nutmeg

¼ teaspoon kosher salt

1 large egg plus 1 egg yolk

1 cup whole milk

½ teaspoon vanilla extract

FOR THE GLAZE

3 cups confectioners' sugar

3 to 5 tablespoons whole milk

1½ tablespoons unsalted butter, melted

½ teaspoon clear vanilla extract

Black food coloring

1. Preheat the oven to 350ºF. Prep a donut pan with non-stick spray.

2. In a bowl, whisk together the flour, sugar, baking powder, nutmeg, and salt.

3. Make a well in the center of the dry ingredients and stir in the egg, egg yolk, milk, and vanilla, until just combined.

4. Pour the batter into a pastry bag and squeeze the batter into the pan until each donut mold is approximately ¾ full.

5. Bake for 14 to 15 minutes. Let cool in the pan for 5 minutes, then transfer to a wire rack.

6. In a small bowl whisk together the confectioners' sugar, milk, melted butter, and clear vanilla. Dip the donuts into the glaze and place on a wire rack to set.

7. To the remaining glaze, stir in the black food coloring. Place into a piping bag and pipe the stormtrooper helmet details onto each donut. When the icing has set, the donuts are ready to serve.

TRIAL 08

STARKILLER ICE TWIST

(GF, V) | Prep time: 5 minutes
Cooking time: N/A | Yield: 1 serving

In an effort to reinforce their supremacy across the galaxy, the First Order creates a gargantuan planet-killing weapon, Starkiller Base. This frosty drink might've been the perfect way for General Hux and Kylo Ren to unwind after a long day of dark side deeds.

¼ cup lemon juice

1 tablespoon granulated sugar

1 cup ice

1½ cups vanilla ice cream

4 twisted lemon peels, to garnish

1. In a blender, add the lemon juice, sugar, and ice. Blend until just combined.
2. Add the vanilla ice cream and blend until smooth.
3. Pour into a glass. Garnish with a twisted lemon peel to serve.

MYNOCK WINGS

(GF) | Prep time: 6 hours
Cooking time: 45 minutes | Yield: 4 servings

The *Millennium Falcon* has a nasty run-in with some mynocks—flying creatures that feed on starships energy. Even though these creatures might look quite scary, they're said to be rather tasty, too—at least according to Rio Durant, an outlaw friend of Han Solo's. Since it'd be best to simply take Rio's word for it, try these citrusy wings instead!

6 pounds chicken wings

¼ cup lemon juice

¼ cup olive oil

2 garlic cloves, minced

1 teaspoon basil

1 teaspoon oregano

½ teaspoon kosher salt

¼ teaspoon black pepper

1. In a sealable bag, add the chicken, lemon juice, olive oil, garlic, basil, oregano, salt, and pepper. Marinate for 6 hours in the refrigerator.
2. Preheat the oven to 400ºF. Place a wire rack onto a baking sheet and grease with non-stick spray.
3. Place the chicken onto the prepped baking sheet. Bake for 45 minutes, until cooked through.

JEDI OUTPOST TUBERS

(GF, V, V+) | Prep time: 10 minutes
Cooking time: 15 minutes | Yield: 6 servings

Jedi of the High Republic stationed on remote worlds would need a hearty meal. In a similar way, this jeera aloo is sure to provide the energy any young chef needs to get through a busy school day!

DID YOU KNOW?

Despite their ordinary appearance, potatoes pack a powerful punch of nutrition. In fact, they contain more potassium and vitamin C per square inch than bananas! Many of their nutrients are contained in the skin, so peeling potatoes takes away some nutritional value. Because potatoes don't have much flavor, cooks like to dress them up with salt, fats, and spices such as cumin.

A LEGENDARY JEDI MASTER

Porter Engle is one of the most famous Jedi of the High Republic era, known for his skill with a lightsaber. However, in his retirement, Porter becomes renowned for another skill entirely—cooking! After all, even Jedi Masters need a hobby.

---

5 medium Yukon gold potatoes, peeled and cubed

2 tablespoons olive oil

2 teaspoons cumin seeds

2 cloves garlic, minced

¾ teaspoon kosher salt

½ teaspoon cumin

½ teaspoon garam masala

½ teaspoon turmeric powder

¼ teaspoon paprika

2 tablespoons water

¼ cup chopped cilantro

---

1. In a large pot over medium high heat, add the potatoes and enough water to cover them by an inch. Bring to a boil, then reduce heat to low, and simmer for 10 minutes until fork tender. Drain and set aside.

2. In a skillet over medium heat, add the olive oil and heat the cumin seeds and garlic, cooking for 1 to 2 minutes, until fragrant. Stir in the salt, cumin, garam masala, turmeric, and paprika. Add water, and cook for 30 seconds, until thickened.

3. Add the potatoes and gently toss with the spices. Cover and cook for 2 minutes more. Add the chopped cilantro before serving.

FRUIT TIE FIGHTERS

(GF, V, V+) | Prep time: 15 minutes
Cooking time: N/A | Yield: 2 servings

TIE fighters are fearsome ships employed by both the Galactic Empire and the dastardly First Order. TIEs often swarm their enemies with powerful cannons and swift speed. Thanks to some tangy apples, this fruity treat packs a similar punch.

DID YOU KNOW?

Each time an apple is cut, oxygen in the air interacts with chemicals in the flesh of the fruit and the apple starts to turn brown. This color transformation is caused by a chemical compound in apples called polyphenol oxidase (poly-fee-nahl ox-ih-dase), or PPO. PPO changes some of the chemicals in the apple into melanin, which contains iron and looks brown. Scientists call this process "oxidative browning." Coating apples with sugar or lemon juice slows down the color change by limiting oxygen exposure and slowing PPO activity.

2 large Granny Smith green apples

2 kiwi

ADDITIONAL SUPPLIES

6 toothpicks

1. Slice and cut the apples into twelve hexagon shapes. Set aside.

2. Peel the kiwi and slice into six ½-inch thick rounds. Poke a toothpick lengthwise through the kiwi round. Skewer a slice of apple onto both ends, so the TIE fighter stands up by itself. Repeat with the remaining apples and kiwi to form six TIE fighters.

LOTH-CAT COOKIES

(GF, V) | Prep time: 20 minutes
Cooking time: 14 minutes | Yield: 12 cookies

Loth-cats may look adorable at first glance, but don't underestimate them—these feisty creatures are skilled at hunting down prey with their sharp teeth and claws. But, unlike loth-cats, these cookies are just as sweet as they appear, exploding with a vibrant burst of chocolatey flavor when you take a bite.

FOR THE COOKIE

12 ounces almond paste

½ cup granulated sugar

½ cup almond flour

¼ teaspoon cinnamon

1 large egg white

1 teaspoon vanilla extract

FOR THE DECORATION

4 ounces dark chocolate, chopped

1. Preheat the oven to 350ºF. Prep baking sheets with parchment.

2. In the bowl of an electric mixer, stir together almond paste, sugar, almond flour, and cinnamon.

3. Stir in the egg white and vanilla.

4. Take 1 tablespoon of dough and form a flattened ball for the face. Place onto the prepped baking sheet. Then take another tablespoon of dough, divide it in half and create two ears, pointed at the ends. Place on top of the flattened ball of dough. Use the back of a knife's blade to create the line of the mouth.

5. Bake for 12 to 14 minutes, until lightly browned. Let cool on a wire rack.

6. Melt the chocolate in a double boiler. Use a small spoon to create the loth-cat markings on the ears, and to create the eyes.

7. When the chocolate has set, the cookies are ready to serve.

TRIAL

09

BOBA'S BOBA

(GF, V, V+) | Prep time: 30 minutes
Cooking time: 1 hour | Yield: 1 serving

One of the most infamous bounty hunters in the galaxy, Boba Fett, uses his skills to capture targets for organizations like the Galactic Empire—for a price, of course! This bright green and red slush salutes Boba Fett's unique Mandalorian armor, and the tapioca pearls hidden inside are delightful little treasures that any bounty hunter would love to get their hands on.

DID YOU KNOW?

A liquid's density depends on how many chemicals are packed into a certain volume of liquid. For example, the more sugar molecules are packed into a cup of water, the denser it will be. Less dense fluids float on top of denser ones, making it possible to create layers of sugary syrup called a "density gradient," like the one you'll make in this recipe.

FOR THE BOBA SIMPLE SYRUP

1 cup water

½ cup brown sugar

½ cup granulated sugar

FOR THE BOBA

2½ cups water

¼ cup boba pearls

FOR THE DRINK

¼ cup frozen green grapes

¼ cup frozen raspberries

¼ cup balled honeydew

1 kiwi, peeled and diced

¼ cup white grape juice

1 cup lemon lime soda

1. For the simple syrup, in a small saucepan over high heat, bring 1 cup water, brown sugar, and granulated sugar to a boil for 2 minutes, until the sugars have dissolved. Let cool.

2. In a large saucepan bring 2½ cups water to a boil. Add the boba pearls, turn down the heat and simmer for 25 minutes. Turn off the heat. Cover the saucepan and let sit for another 25 minutes.

3. Drain and rinse the boba pearls, then pour into the cooled simple syrup. Let soak for 30 minutes.

4. Scoop the boba pearls out of simple syrup and spoon into a tall glass. Add the frozen grapes, frozen raspberries, kiwi, and honeydew.

5. Pour over the white grape juice and lemon lime soda.

6. Add a boba straw to serve.

BB-8 SLURRY

[GF, V] | Prep time: 5 minutes
Cooking time: N/A | Yield: 1 serving

With its orange and white colors, this creamy, sparkling drink celebrates the sweet personality of BB-8, one of the bravest droids of the Resistance.

1 cup lemon lime soda

¼ cup orange juice

⅛ teaspoon clear vanilla extract

1 scoop orange sherbet

1 scoop vanilla ice cream

1 orange slice, for garnish

1. Pour the lemon lime soda, orange juice, and vanilla into a tall glass. Stir.

2. Add a scoop of orange sherbet and a scoop of vanilla ice cream.

3. Garnish with the orange slice before serving.

DID YOU KNOW?

Carbon dioxide (CO_2) is everywhere and is one of the gases that makes up Earth's atmosphere. Humans exhale it as we breathe, and large amounts of the gas are produced when we burn fossil fuels like oil and coal. Carbon dioxide is also the gas that makes soda fizzy. Carbonated drinks are made of water, sugary syrup, flavoring, and carbon dioxide gas bubbles. Today, factories make carbonated beverages by dissolving carbon dioxide gas into cold water.

A TRUSTY DROID

Just before being captured by Kylo Ren, Poe Dameron entrusts BB-8 with top secret information—the missing piece of a map that would lead to Luke Skywalker. BB-8 is just as instrumental to the Resistance's fight against the First Order as any of its heroes, from Leia Organa to Rey.

JAR JAR'S JACKFRUIT STEW

(GF, V, V+) | Prep time: 20 minutes
Cooking time: 1 hour 15 minutes | Yield: 6 servings

This rich, filling stew is packed with strong flavors, which are owed to the use of jackfruit. Since the Gungan home world of Naboo is a planet rich with all types of flora, this jackfruit stew would be right at home in any Gungan dinner table, maybe even Jar Jar Binks's. Pretty soon, you'll be saying, "Mesa want seconds!"

DID YOU KNOW?

Jackfruit is a huge, spined, oval fruit. Considered the largest fruit in the world grown on a tree, jackfruits can weigh from 10 to 100 pounds. Canned green jackfruit, nicknamed a "vegetable meat," has a mild flavor and meat-like texture. When fruits and vegetables such as jackfruit are cooked, they lose crispness and become tender as cells and cell membranes are broken down.

- 2 cans (20 ounces) young green jackfruit
- 2 tablespoons olive oil
- 1 sweet onion, sliced
- 2 large celery ribs, cut into chunks
- 2 large carrots, cut into chunks
- 1 large orange bell pepper, cut into chunks
- 2 garlic cloves, minced
- 1 tablespoon light brown sugar
- 1 tablespoon dried oregano
- 1 tablespoon dried thyme
- ½ teaspoon paprika
- ½ teaspoon kosher salt
- ½ teaspoon black pepper
- 1 bay leaf
- 1 can (28 ounces) diced tomatoes
- 1 tablespoon tomato paste
- 32 ounces vegetable broth
- 1 tablespoon Worcestershire sauce
- 1 can (14 ounces) coconut milk
- 2 tablespoons minced fresh parsley

1. Drain and rinse jackfruit and then squeeze out the water. Cut the jackfruit into smaller pieces and remove the core. Set aside.

2. In a Dutch oven, heat the olive oil over medium high heat. Add the onion, celery, carrots, bell pepper, and garlic. Cook for 2 to 3 minutes until softened.

3. Add the jackfruit, brown sugar, oregano, thyme, paprika, salt, pepper, and bay leaf. Cook for another 2 to 3 minutes.

4. Add the tomatoes, tomato paste, vegetable broth, and Worcestershire sauce. Bring to a boil.

5. Lower heat to low. Cover and simmer for one hour.

6. Stir in the coconut milk and simmer for 5 minutes, until the stew has thickened slightly.

7. Discard the bay leaf. Garnish with parsley to serve.

PADAWAN BRAIDED BREAD

[V] | Prep time: 3 hours

Cooking time: 20 minutes | Yield: 10 servings

Padawans wear braids in their hair to signify the fact that they're still in training. Both Obi-Wan Kenobi and Anakin Skywalker sported braids during their tenure as Padawans. As Padawans move up the ranks and become a Jedi Knight, they're allowed to shed their braids—but this beautifully braided bread is so tasty, you just might want to put off passing the Jedi Trials for a while!

¾ cup warm whole milk, 110ºF

1 envelope (2¼ teaspoons) dry yeast

2¼ cups all-purpose flour

2 tablespoons honey

1 teaspoon kosher salt

1 large egg

1 tablespoon olive oil, for greasing

1 large egg yolk plus 1 tablespoon water, for egg wash

2 tablespoons sesame seeds

1. In the bowl of an electric mixer, sprinkle the yeast over the warm milk and let sit for 5 minutes, until foamy.

2. Add the flour, honey, salt, and egg, kneading for 5 minutes until smooth and elastic. Place the dough into a large bowl greased with oil, turning to coat. Cover with plastic wrap and let rise for two hours, until doubled in size.

3. Punch down the dough, then turn out onto a lightly floured surface. Cut dough into 10 equal pieces.

4. Roll out one piece into a 6-by-4-inch rectangle. Make two lengthwise cuts, dividing the dough into three strips. Braid the strips together, tucking the ends under, to seal. Transfer to a baking sheet lined with parchment. Repeat with the remaining dough. Cover with a clean kitchen towel and let rise again for 30 minutes.

5. Preheat the oven to 350ºF. In a small bowl, whisk the egg yolk and water. Brush the rolls with the egg wash. Sprinkle with **sesame** seeds.

6. Bake for 20 minutes until golden brown. Let cool on a wire rack.

"MAY THE FILLING BE WITH YOU" CUPCAKES

[V] | Prep time: 1 hour
Cooking time: 20 minutes | Yield: 18 cupcakes

These cupcakes may seem similar, but that doesn't mean they're identical. Biting into a cupcake displays luscious filling that's either red or blue. The color you get will reveal whether the light side of the Force is strong within you, like the heroes Luke Skywalker and Rey, or if you fit in better with dark side acolytes like Kylo Ren and Darth Maul. Either way, as you embark on your baking journey, may the Force (and delicious filling) be with you!

DID YOU KNOW?

Eggs are a key ingredient when baking cakes. The proteins in eggs form bubbles when you whip them, adding structure to the cake. They also supply water that turns to steam, allowing the cake to puff up even higher. While flour, sugar, and eggs form the scaffolding of cake, fats like oil and butter help to stabilize the edible architecture of a cake.

FOR THE CUPCAKES

2 cups all-purpose flour

2 tablespoons cocoa powder

½ teaspoon baking powder

¼ teaspoon kosher salt

½ cup semi-sweet chocolate chips, melted

½ cup (1 stick) unsalted butter

1½ cups granulated sugar

2 large eggs

1 teaspoon vanilla extract

1 cup chocolate milk

FOR THE FILLING

One 8-ounce package cream cheese

1 cup powdered sugar

½ teaspoon vanilla extract

¼ teaspoon kosher salt

Blue food gel dye

Red food gel dye

FOR THE FROSTING

1 cup (2 sticks) unsalted butter, softened

4 cups confectioners' sugar

1 teaspoon vanilla extract

4 to 6 tablespoons whole milk, as needed

3 tablespoons dark cocoa powder

2 teaspoons edible pearl luster dust

CONTINUED ON PAGE 110

1. Preheat the oven to 350ºF. Prep a cupcake pan with liners.

2. In a medium bowl, whisk together the flour, cocoa powder, baking powder, and salt. Set aside.

3. In the bowl of an electric mixer beat the melted chocolate, butter, and sugar. Add the eggs and the vanilla, until just combined.

4. Alternate the flour mixture and the chocolate milk, until combined.

5. Fill the liners two-thirds full and bake for 17 to 19 minutes, depending on your oven. Let cool on a wire rack.

6. Use a paring knife to core and remove the centers of the cupcakes.

7. In the bowl of an electric mixer combine the cream cheese, powdered sugar, vanilla and salt. Stir well until combined. Divide equally into two bowls.

8. Use the red food gel dye to color one bowl of cream cheese filling red. Use the blue food gel dye to color the second bowl blue.

9. Scoop the fillings into two separate piping bags. Randomly pipe the fillings into the centers of the cupcakes. Place cupcakes in the refrigerator.

10. In the bowl of an electric mixer, cream the butter while adding the confectioners' sugar a little at a time.

11. Add the vanilla and milk. Turn the mixer up to medium high and whip for 10 to 15 seconds.

12. Take half the frosting and place into one small disposable piping bag, set aside.

13. Place the remaining frosting into a medium bowl. Add the dark cocoa powder, stirring until combined.

14. Then scoop the chocolate frosting into a second small disposable piping bag.

15. Use scissors to snip holes in the bottoms of both bags. Insert both bags into a larger (16-inch) disposable piping bag fitted with a decorative star tip.

16. Pipe the two-tone frosting onto the cupcakes, covering the cream cheese filling.

17. Sprinkle with edible luster dust to serve.

TRIAL
10

SARLACC SHAKE

(V) | Prep time: 15 minutes

Cooking time: 10 minutes | Yield: 1 serving

The sarlacc is a massive creature that can be found in the deserts of Tatooine. A sarlacc nests in the sand, with its beaky mouth and tentacles rising to form a pit of sorts. Anyone unfortunate enough to fall into a sarlacc pit is digested in the beast's belly for a thousand years. Just in case you've got the appetite of a sarlacc, you'll be able to whip up a sweet treat with this chocolate shake!

FOR THE PASTRY

1 sheet (7 ounces) pre-made pie dough

1 large egg plus 1 tablespoon water, for egg wash

1 teaspoon sanding sugar

FOR THE SHAKE

3 cups chocolate ice cream

1 cup chocolate milk

2 tablespoons chocolate syrup

1. Preheat oven to 450ºF. Prep a baking sheet with parchment paper.

2. Roll out the pie dough. Cut two petal-shaped pieces and then cut the rest of the dough into long strips. Twist to create tentacles. Place onto the prepped baking sheet.

3. Brush the pieces with eggs wash and sprinkle with sanding sugar.

4. Bake for 10 to 12 minutes, until golden brown. Let cool on a wire rack.

5. In a blender, add the chocolate ice cream, chocolate milk, and chocolate syrup. Blend until smooth.

6. Pour into a tall glass. Add the sarlacc and tentacles to serve.

NABOO SHEPHERD'S PIE

Prep time: 20 minutes

Cooking time: 50 minutes | Yield: 10 servings

NABOO

The farmers on the noble planet Naboo often herd shaak, gentle animals that graze on the planet's grassy plains. This rich, potato-topped meat pie would be a favorite dish on the farms!

FOR THE MASHED POTATOES

3 russet potatoes, peeled and quartered

⅔ cup heavy cream

4 tablespoons unsalted butter

1 teaspoon kosher salt

¼ teaspoon white pepper

FOR THE FILLING

2 tablespoons unsalted butter

2 tablespoons olive oil

1 medium onion, diced

2 medium carrots, peeled and diced

2 ribs celery, diced

6 ounces brown mushrooms, quartered

6 ounces white mushrooms, quartered

2 garlic cloves, minced

1 pound ground beef

½ pound ground lamb

1 tablespoon Worcestershire sauce

2 tablespoons tomato paste

1 teaspoon oregano

1 teaspoon parsley

1 teaspoon thyme

½ teaspoon onion powder

½ teaspoon paprika

½ teaspoon kosher salt

¼ teaspoon black pepper

1 tablespoon cornstarch

2 tablespoon water

FOR THE TOPPING

3 tablespoons grated Parmesan

2 tablespoons unsalted butter, cubed

1. Place potatoes in a large pot and cover with water. Over high heat, bring to a boil and then reduce to a simmer and cook for 12 minutes, until tender. Drain, do not rinse.

2. Return potatoes to pot and mash with heavy cream and butter. Season with salt and white pepper. Set aside.

3. Preheat the oven to 375ºF.

4. In a large skillet, heat the butter and olive oil. Add the onion, carrots, celery, mushrooms, and garlic. Cook for 10 minutes, until softened.

5. Add the ground beef and ground lamb, cooking for 4 to 5 minutes until no longer pink. Stir in the Worcestershire sauce, tomato paste, oregano, parsley, thyme, onion powder, paprika, salt, and pepper.

6. In a small bowl stir together the cornstarch and water. Stir into the pan and cook for 1 minute until the beef and lamb mixture is slightly thickened.

7. Spoon the filling into a deep 9-by-9-inch baking dish. Top with the mashed potatoes, leaving space around the edges. Sprinkle with Parmesan cheese and dot with butter.

8. Bake for 30 minutes. Let cool slightly and serve.

SCAVENGER SCONES

[V] | Prep time: 10 minutes
Cooking time: 20 minutes | Yield: 10 servings

As a scavenger on the desert planet of Jakku, Rey trades machine parts for portion bread—a substance that instantly expands into bread, when combined with water. Life on Jakku is tough, and so portion bread likely isn't very tasty. With this cheese-filled scone recipe, you'll learn to create a yummier version of that Jakku staple.

2 cups all-purpose flour

1 tablespoon baking powder

2 teaspoons granulated sugar

1 teaspoon dried mustard

¼ teaspoon kosher salt

½ cup (1 stick) unsalted cold butter, cubed

½ cup heavy cream, plus 2 tablespoons for glazing

1 cup shredded cheddar cheese

½ cup shredded Monterey jack cheese

1. Preheat the oven to 400ºF. Prep a baking sheet with parchment paper.

2. In a bowl whisk together flour, baking powder, sugar, dried mustard, and salt. Set aside.

3. Work the butter into the flour mixture, until crumbly. Add ½ cup heavy cream.

4. Fold in the cheese.

5. Onto a floured surface, pat out the dough to ¾-inch thick. Use a 2-inch round cutter to cut out circles and place onto the prepped baking sheet. Brush with remaining 2 tablespoons of heavy cream.

6. Bake for 18 minutes until golden brown.

JEDI TEMPLE SALAD

[V] | Prep time: 15 minutes
Cooking time: N/A | Yield: 6 servings

The Jedi Temple on Coruscant is the central hub of the Jedi Order. It is where the Jedi Council convenes and where the Order's archives are stored. For many living on Coruscant, the Temple's towers are a symbol of peace and justice. For you, this salad's towers of lavash will be a symbol of nutrition and fulfillment!

DID YOU KNOW?

Cabbage looks a lot like lettuce, but it is actually a member of the brassica genus of plants, which includes other cruciferous vegetables like broccoli, cauliflower, mustard, and kale. The word cruciferous comes from the Latin word for cross, because cruciferous vegetables have flowers with four petals, which can be found in a cross-like fashion. High in fiber and rich in nutrients, cabbage and related vegetables have a strong smell because they contain sulfur. Some scientists believe that certain chemical compounds called phytochemicals found in cruciferous plants may help prevent disease in humans who eat them. In nature, phytochemicals repel insects and animals and help plants fight infection from microbes such as bacteria, viruses, and fungi.

FOR THE DRESSING

⅓ cup mayonnaise

1 tablespoon apple cider vinegar

2 teaspoons Dijon mustard

1 teaspoon lemon juice

1 teaspoon granulated sugar

½ teaspoon kosher salt

½ teaspoon black pepper

FOR THE SALAD

8 cups shredded green cabbage

1 Granny Smith apple, cored and sliced

½ cup sliced almonds

½ cup pomegranate seeds

½ cup thinly sliced red onion

5 pieces lavash crackers, for garnish

1. In a small bowl whisk together the mayonnaise, apple cider vinegar, Dijon mustard, lemon juice, sugar, salt, and pepper. Set aside.

2. In a large bowl toss the cabbage, apples, almonds, pomegranate seeds, and onion. Fold in the dressing.

3. Stand the 5 lavash crackers upright in the bowl, to serve.

KYBER CRYSTAL CANDY

[GF, V, V+] | Prep time: 20 minutes
Cooking time: 50 minutes | Yield: 10 servings

A hallmark of any Jedi's training is the construction of their lightsaber. This long-held tradition begins with finding a kyber crystal, which powers a lightsaber, and gives the blade its color. Yoda often guides younglings to the planet Ilum, where the Jedi-in-training enter the planet's complex system of caves, seeking out the unique kyber crystal that calls to them personally. Even though you might find it difficult to travel to the planet Ilum, don't worry—with this recipe, you'll be able to create your own kyber crystal (albeit in candy form)!

FOR THE CANDY

1 cup water

3 cups granulated sugar plus 1 tablespoon for rolling skewers

3 to 4 drops food coloring (blue, green, yellow, purple, white, or red)

½ teaspoon candy flavoring oil (flavor of choice)

ADDITIONAL SUPPLIES

6-to-8-inch skewers

Clothespins

1 clean Mason jar

Coffee filter

Rubber band

CONTINUED ON PAGE 123

1. Wet skewer with water, then roll in granulated sugar, leaving at least 2 inches bare to use as a handle. Set aside to dry completely. Crystals will grow from the skewer.

2. Fasten a clothespin horizontally across the bare end of the skewer, so that the skewer looks like a "T." Rest skewer in the jar such that the clothespin spans the top of the jar. If the skewer reaches the bottom of the jar, make sure to trim it or the crystal will get stuck to the bottom.

3. In a medium saucepan over medium-high heat, bring water to a boil. Add ½ cup of sugar at a time, stirring until completely dissolved before adding the next ½ cup. After sugar has dissolved, stir in the food coloring and flavored oil.

4. Carefully pour hot sugar solution into jar until skewer is covered. Top with a coffee filter and fasten with a rubber band, to cover. Allow the mixture to cool before moving to a cool dry place out of direct sunlight.

5. Crystals take about 7 days to fully form. If a layer of crystal has built up around the top of the jar, gently break with a spoon before removing your grown crystals.

6. Once grown, transfer the crystal to an empty glass and allow it to drip dry.

7. Remove the crystal from the skewer, by breaking it apart.

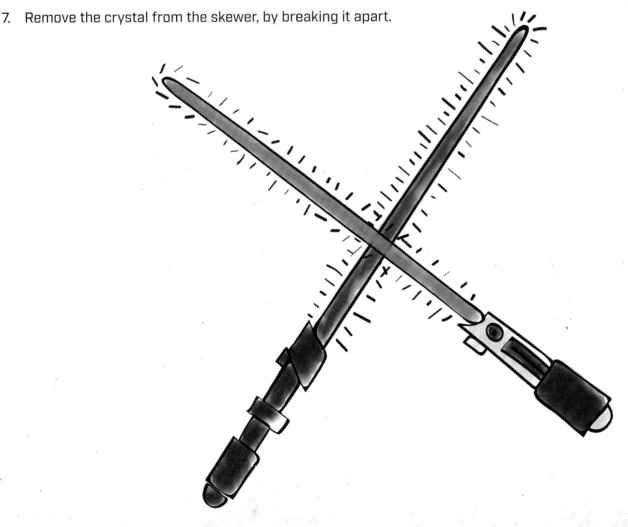

GLOSSARY

ACID: Acids are sour-tasting chemicals that can be dissolved in water and react with chemicals called bases to form salts.

ATMOSPHERE: The layer of gases enveloping certain planets.

ATOM: Made of particles called electrons, protons, and neutrons, atoms are the smallest pieces of matter and are the building blocks of everything on Earth.

BACTERIA: Single-celled organisms that can be seen only under a microscope and grow almost everywhere on Earth.

BOND/BIND: Chemical bonds involve a strong attractive force holding atoms together.

CARBONATED: Containing carbon dioxide gas bubbles.

CARBON: A chemical element. All living things on Earth contain carbon.

CARBOHYDRATE: Large carbon-containing molecules, composed of sugars and fibers and found in foods including fruits, vegetables, grains, nuts, beans, and dairy products.

CARBON DIOXIDE: A heavy, colorless gas often used to carbonate beverages.

CARTILAGE: A strong, flexible tissue serving multiple purposes in humans and other animals.

CELL: The basic unit of life, composed of genetic material such as DNA and other cellular machinery contained inside of a cell membrane.

CELL MEMBRANE: An ultra-thin layer separating the contents of a cell from its environment. Cell membranes allow the movement of certain small molecules in and out of the cell.

CELLULOSE: A substance that makes up plant cell walls and that cannot be dissolved by water.

CELL WALL: A rigid layer found just outside the cell membrane of the cells of plants, fungi, and bacteria.

CELSIUS: Scale for measuring temperature in which water freezes at 0 degrees and boils at 100 degrees.

CHEMICAL: Substance made up of a particular group of molecules.

CHROMOSOMES: Thread-like structures composed of DNA and proteins and found in a compartment inside plant and animal cells called the nucleus.

COMPOUND: A chemical substance made up of two or more elements bonded together in certain proportions.

CRYSTAL: A solid compound with a consistent three-dimensional pattern of atoms or molecules and a smooth surface. Sugar, diamonds, and salt are all crystals.

DENSITY: A measure of how many molecules are packed into a certain amount of space.

DNA (DEOXYRIBONUCLEIC ACID): A molecule shaped like a twisted ladder. Found in the cells of living organisms, DNA carries genetic information required for life.

ENERGY: The potential to do work or produce heat.

ENZYME: Proteins within living cells that speed up chemical reactions and can quickly break chemical bonds.

EVAPORATE: The process of changing from a liquid to a gas.

FAHRENHEIT: A temperature scale based on 32 degrees as the freezing point of water and 212 degrees as the boiling point.

FATS: A compound containing fatty acids, which is found in animals and used to store energy.

FERMENTATION: A series of chemical reactions producing energy. Microorganisms ferment food to produce special food products, including kimchi, pickles, yogurt, certain cheeses, and alcoholic beverages.

FIBER: The components of fruits and vegetables that humans can't digest. Fiber helps move food through the digestive tract and supports a healthy microbe population in the gut.

FUNGI: A group of living organisms including bread yeast, mushrooms, molds, and mildew.

GAS: One of four states of matter. Gas particles carry lots of kinetic energy (the energy of motion) and are in constant motion. Packed so loosely that they have no defined shape or volume, gas particles will spread out indefinitely if they are not contained.

GELATIN: A see-through, colorless ingredient made from collagen and used to thicken foods and create gels.

GENUS: A group of related organisms of the same family, containing one or more species.

GLUTEN: A group of proteins found in edible grasses, including wheat, barley, and rye. Gluten helps dough rise and gives baked goods shape and a chewy texture.

HYDRATE: To cause to absorb water.

HYDROCOLLOID: Substance that forms a gel in the presence of water. Hydrocolloids are often used to thicken foods and improve their texture.

HYDRODYNAMICS: The study of liquids in motion.

LEAVEN: To cause dough or bread to rise by adding yeast or another ingredient that adds bubbles.

LIQUID: A substance such as water that flows freely and takes on the shape of its container, but maintains its volume.

MATTER: Anything that takes up space.

MICROBIOME: The collection of all the microorganisms in a certain environment, such as the digestive tract of a human.

MICROORGANISMS: Bacteria, fungi, viruses, and other organisms too small to see without a microscope. Often called microbes.

MINERAL: A naturally occurring solid with a well-defined chemical composition and a regular structure.

MOLECULE: Two or more atoms held together by chemical bonds.

NUTRITION: A branch of science that deals with the food necessary for health and growth.

OPAQUE: Something you cannot see through.

ORGANIC: Relating to living matter, which contains compounds made of carbon. Organic foods are produced without the use of chemicals considered harmful to humans and the environment.

PARTICLES: Small objects with chemical or physical properties.

PIGMENT: A chemical substance that gives color to other materials.

PRESERVATIVE: Chemicals that prevent spoilage by bacteria, fungi, and viruses.

PROTEIN: Encoded by DNA, proteins are large molecules made up of one or more long chains of amino acids. Proteins are essential components of muscle, hair, antibodies, and enzymes.

REACTION: In chemistry, a process in which one or more substances come into contact with each other, and the atoms or molecules are recombined to form new things.

RECEPTORS: Structures including molecules, cells, and sensory organs that receive signals from the environment.

RIPE/RIPEN: To develop a certain smell, flavor, and texture.

SOLID: One of four states of matter. In solids, particles do not have much kinetic energy (the energy of motion), but have a fixed position, and are tightly packed together so they cannot move very much.

SOLUTION: A mixture of two or more substances—the thing that is dissolved (solute) and the thing it is dissolved in (solvent).

STARCH: Long chains of linked sugar molecules made by plants to store energy.

SUGARS: Carbon-containing molecules used by living things as a source of energy.

TISSUE: The material animals and plants are made of, often a group of similar cells with similar function, such as muscle tissue.

TRANSLUCENT: Allowing light to pass through, but not completely transparent (clear).

VITAMINS: Chemical compounds required for growth and nutrition.

VOLUME: The amount of space that something takes up.

YEAST: A living microorganism related to mushrooms. Bread yeast (baker's yeast) eats the carbohydrates in grains like wheat to form carbon dioxide gas bubbles, causing bread dough to rise.

ABOUT THE AUTHORS

Jenn Fujikawa is the lifestyle and pop culture author of *Star Wars: The Life Day Cookbook: Official Holiday Recipes from a Galaxy Far, Far Away*; *Gudetama: The Official Cookbook: Recipes for Living a Lazy Life*; *The I Love Lucy Cookbook: Classic Recipes Inspired by the Iconic TV Show*; and *The Goldbergs Cookbook*. She has created content for Disney, Ghostbusters, Lucasfilm, Marvel, and more. As a contributing author to the official *Star Wars* website, she has created more than 120 recipes on starwars.com. Unique family dinners and geeky baking are a staple of her website www.justjennrecipes.com.

Liz Lee Heinecke has been a Star Wars fan since the 1970s, when she stood in line to get Darth Vader's autograph, traded Star Wars cards with her sister, and listened to the original Star Wars soundtrack on vinyl. Today, with ten years of molecular biology research and a master's degree in bacteriology under her belt, Liz regularly shares her enthusiasm for Star Wars and science on www.kitchenpantryscientist.com, TV, social media, and in her books: *Star Wars Maker Lab*, *Kitchen Science Lab for Kids*, *Outdoor Science Lab for Kids*, *STEAM Lab for Kids*, *Kitchen Science Lab for Kids—Edible Edition*, *The Kitchen Pantry Scientist: Chemistry for Kids*, *The Kitchen Pantry Scientist: Biology for Kids*, *The Kitchen Pantry Scientist: Physics for Kids*, *Sheet Pan Science*, and *RADIANT: The Dancer, The Scientist and a Friendship Forged in Light*. Most days, you'll find Liz at home in Minnesota, reading, writing, creating science experiments, singing, and occasionally playing the banjo.

ACKNOWLEDGMENTS

❝ *Sometimes it takes courage to stick to one's beliefs, young Padawan.* ❞

—Aayla Secura

I've had the pleasure of cooking so many meals and treats for my family and my friends' kids over the years. This book is for them: Tyler & Mason, Aidan & Gwen, Kolten, Penelope & Hannah, Kai & Kekoa & Kamaka, Joy & Kaylin, Michael & Anne, Isabela R., Isabela S. & Lily, Tyler S., Ava W., Holden & Riley, Aaron & Casiel & Emmett, Hazel B., Brandon & Caitlyn, Spencer B., Jacob E., Tora M., Mason S., Henry & Gracie, Major & Parker, and many more. I hope all of you younglings grow up to be everything you want to be. May the Force be with you.

Jenn Fujikawa

❝ *I don't believe in being interested in a subject just because it's said to be important. I believe in being caught by it somehow or other.* ❞

—Joseph Campbell, *The Power of Myth*

To my parents, Ron and Jean, and my sister Karin, who sat beside me in 1977 when I fell head over heels into Star Wars, and to Ken, Charlie, May, and Sarah, who continue to explore that expanding universe with me today.

Liz Lee Heinecke

INSIGHT
EDITIONS

PO Box 3088
San Rafael, CA 94912

www.insighteditions.com

Find us on Facebook: www.facebook.com/InsightEditions

Follow us on Twitter: @insighteditions

Library of Congress Cataloging-in-Publication Data available.

ISBN: 978-1-64722-631-2

Publisher: Raoul Goff
VP of Licensing and Partnerships: Vanessa Lopez
VP of Creative: Chrissy Kwasnik
VP of Manufacturing: Alix Nicholaeff
Editorial Director: Vicki Jaeger
Designer: Brooke McCullum
Editor: Harrison Tunggal
Editorial Assistant: Grace Orriss
Production Associate: Deena Hashem
Senior Production Manager, Subsidiary Rights: Lina s Palma

Kyber Crystal Candy recipe by August Craig

Photography: Ted Thomas
Food and Prop Styling: Elena P Craig
Food and Prop Styling Assistant: August Craig

Special thanks to Albin Johnson.

FOR LUCASFILM:
Senior Editor: Robert Simpson
Creative Director of Publishing: Michael Siglain
Art Director: Troy Alders
Lucasfilm Story Group: Emily Shkoukani, Kelsey Sharpe
Creative Art Manager: Phil Szostak

Learn more about R2-KT and her mission to spread hope by visiting www.r2kt.com.

ROOTS of PEACE   REPLANTED PAPER

Insight Editions, in association with Roots of Peace, will plant two trees for each tree used in the manufacturing of this book. Roots of Peace is an internationally renowned humanitarian organization dedicated to eradicating land mines worldwide and converting war-torn lands into productive farms and wildlife habitats. Roots of Peace will plant two million fruit and nut trees in Afghanistan and provide farmers there with the skills and support necessary for sustainable land use.

Manufactured in Turkey by Insight Editions

10 9 8 7 6 5 4 3 2 1